BEARS in the WOODS

QUILT

a Quilt in a Day® Publication

For Sue, and the Dream we shared.

If the moon and stars call you their friend,

May the dreams that you share with them never end.

Author Unknown

First printing October, 1997

Published by Quilt in a Day®, Inc.
1955 Diamond St. San Marcos, CA 92069

©1997 by Eleanor Burns Family Trust

ISBN 0-922705-95-X

Editor Eleanor Burns
Assistant Editor Susan Bouchard
Art Director Merritt Voigtlander

Table of Contents

Introduction 4

   Fabric Selection 6

   Supplies 7

   Bears in the Woods Quilt Yardage 8

   Cutting Strips 10

   Cutting Squares and Rectangles 11

   Pressing and Applique 12

   Practice Blocks .14

Log Cabin Block (Full size & Wallhanging) 16

   Timber Line 12 Block Log Cabin 32

   Mantle Cover .34

   16 Block Log Cabin Projects 36

Tree Block (Full size & Wallhanging) 40

   Twenty Block Tree Quilt 56

   Twelve Block Tree Quilt 57

   Caribou Crossing 58

   Tree Ornaments 61

   Tablecloth or Tree Skirt 64

Bear's Paw (Full size & Wallhanging) 70

   Bear's Paw Wallhanging 80

   Bear Valley Wallhanging 82

Flying Geese (Full size & Wallhanging) 92

   Migrating Geese 99

   Cabin in the Pines Wallhanging 104

   Quilt Box 113

Finishing the Quilt 118

Introduction

Since I was young, I've felt I was born in the wrong century. Perhaps I should have been born in the nineteenth century.

I have always imagined myself carving my way through the wilderness. I would scare away the wild animals, and then build a log cabin out of the tallest pines I could find. For Thanksgiving, I'd stir up a big pot of Bear Stew for my sons, Grant and Orion, on the open hearth. On Christmas Day, we'd feast on stuffed goose.

But alas, I was born in 1945, and I missed that whole part of our country's history. As least, I can study the legacy left behind in the settlers' quilts. The quilt patterns and their names tell the story.

Sue Bouchard designed this quilt using **four of their basic blocks** to help tell that story of long ago, including Log Cabin, Pine Tree, Bears Paw and Flying Geese blocks. **Twelve Log Cabin blocks** make up the center of the Bears in the Woods quilt, with traditional red centers and scrappy looking logs. It was the Pennsylvania Germans who were responsible for the adoption of the log cabin by American settlers. At least, I am Pennsylvania German!

The settlers were grateful for the pines. The tall straight trunks saved them many hours when constructing their log home, as logs were easily notched and layered together. In this quilt, **twenty Tree blocks** in varying shades of green are refreshing.

Perhaps out of fear, the pioneer quiltmaker designed the first Bear's Paw blocks. For certain, I would be respectful of the bears and dedicate a quilt pattern to them! In the quilt, **four Bear's Paw blocks** square the Log Cabin and Tree blocks.

Early settlers didn't need to worry about food, as the skies, lakes, and streams offered plenty of wild foul to eat. In true pioneer spirit, **one hundred and four Flying Geese blocks** flock to the edges of this quilt in a collection of homespun fabrics. You can use the same fabrics you used in your Log Cabin blocks, or dig into your scraps just as the settlers did, and come up with different fabrics.

Sue was inspired to make the Bears in the Woods quilt while vacationing on Ashley Lake in Montana. Sue and I vacationed there in the summer of 1997. Geese were swimming on the clear lake, and in the water's reflection, tall pines stood majestically. Across the way stood a log cabin, abandoned long ago. Although we never saw bears, there were tracks of some sort leading from the water! Scary bears wouldn't dare break the serenity at Ashley Lake!

You can sew the four sets of basic blocks together for a full size Bears in the Woods quilt, or make a wallhanging with pieces one fourth the size, or you can make a basket full of woodsy quilts, using the various blocks. Twelve Log Cabin blocks can be sewn into a traditional lap robe. Twenty Tree blocks make a double bed size quilt, perfect for a country home or mountain retreat. Four Bear's Paw blocks, along with lattice and cornerstones, make a wallhanging just the right size for a country mantel, or a sleeping baby. A twin size quilt can be made from the one hundred four Geese. In plaids and checks, this quilt has masculine appeal. Smaller wallhangings and projects from each one of the blocks are also illustrated.

May you, too, enjoy these traditional patterns from the settlers!

Eleanor Burns

Fabric Selection

The Bears in the Woods Quilt consists of four main blocks, the Log Cabin, Trees, Bear's Paw and Flying Geese. Fabric suggestions for each type of block are provided. Small to medium, traditional type fabrics work well in this quilt.

Log Cabin Block

The center of the Log Cabin Block is traditionally red to represent the warmth and heart of the home. Surrounding the center is the combination of your background fabric and eight different blues.

Tree Block

A selection of ten different greens, with a variety of yellow and blue tints give the Tree Block a very natural feel. Select two wood printed browns for the trunks. Add interest by selecting a variety of light, medium and dark greens.

Bear's Paw Block

A combination of a small brown plaid and a golden brown for the claws gives the block an authentic feel of a bear. Some plaids are directional, so remember this characteristic when assembling your block.

Flying Geese Blocks

The Flying Geese blocks are made from a variety of eight blue small pattern prints. These fabrics may be the same ones used in the Log Cabin Blocks or additional prints may be introduced.

Background

Choose a light neutral fabric that contrasts with the rest of the fabrics selected for the blocks in the quilt. This can be either a tone-on-tone or a very subtle print.

The Yardage Chart for the Full Size and Wallhanging size quilts are located on page 9. Individual cutting charts are provided in the beginning pages of each technique.

Supplies

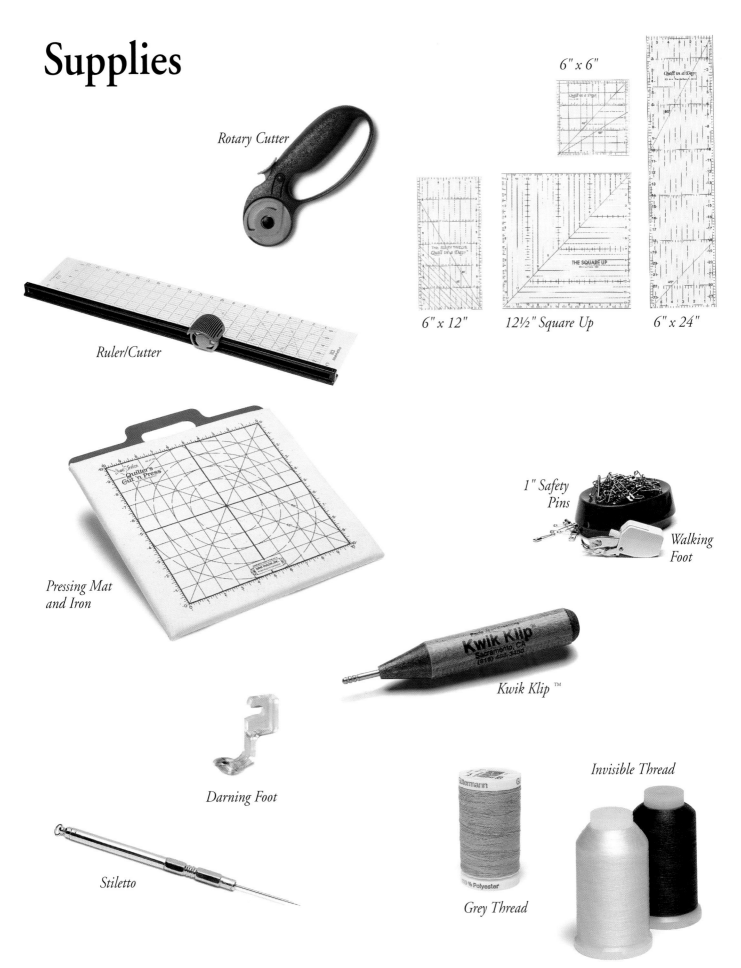

Rotary Cutter

6" x 6"

6" x 12"

12½" Square Up

6" x 24"

Ruler/Cutter

Pressing Mat
and Iron

1" Safety
Pins

Walking
Foot

Kwik Klip ™

Darning Foot

Invisible Thread

Stiletto

Grey Thread

Bears in the Woods Quilt Yardage

Full Size 84" x 84"
Wallhanging 42" x 42"

Additional Yardage Required for Queen/King 96" x 96"

Border (Outside of Flying Geese)	2¼ yds
	(11) 6½" strips
Binding	1 yd
	(11) 3" strips
Batting	102" x 102"
Backing	3 yds (108" wide)

	Full Size 12" Finished Block	Wallhanging 6" Finished Block	Instructions See page…
Background Fabric	6¼ yards	3½ yds	
Twelve Log Cabins			
Center Square	⅛ yd of each	⅛ yd of each	Page 16
First Dark			
Second Dark			
Third Dark			
Fourth Dark	¼ yd of each	⅛ yd of each	
Fifth Dark			
Sixth Dark			
Seventh Dark	⅓ yd of each	⅛ yd of each	
Eighth Dark			
 **Twenty Trees**			
Ten Different Greens	¼ yd of each	⅛ yd of each	Page 41
Two Trunks	⅛ yd of each	⅛ yd of each	
 **Four Bear's Paw**			
Claws	⅜ yd	¼ yd	Page 71
Paws	⅓ yd	⅛ yd	
Center (Same as Log Cabin)	⅛ yd	⅛ yd	
 **One Hundred Four Flying Geese**			
Eight Different Darks	¼ yd of each	⅛ yd of each	Page 93
(May be same as Log Cabin)			
Binding	⅞ yd	½ yd	Finishing Page 118
(May be same as Log Cabin Center)			
Batting	90" x 90"	48" x 48"	
Backing	2½ yds (90" wide)	50" x 50"	

Cutting Strips

Use a large rotary cutter with a sharp blade and a 6" x 24" plexiglass ruler on a gridded cutting mat. Check that the measurements are the same on the ruler and the gridded cutting mat.

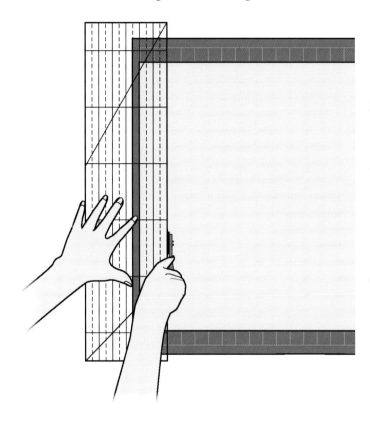

1. Make a nick on the selvage edge, and tear your fabric from selvage to selvage to put the fabric on the straight of the grain.

2. Fold the fabric in half, matching the torn straight edge thread to thread.

3. With the fold of the fabric at the top, line up the torn edge of fabric on the gridded cutting mat with the left edge extended slightly to the left of zero. Reverse this procedure if you are left-handed.

4. Line up the 6" x 24" ruler on zero. Spread the fingers of your left hand to hold the ruler firmly. With the rotary cutter in your right hand, begin cutting off the fabric on the mat. Put all your strength into the rotary cutter as you cut away from you, and trim the torn, ragged edge.

5. Accuracy is important. For blocks: Lift, and move the ruler until it lines up with the strip width on the grid and cut. Refer to your Yardage Chart.

6. Open the first strip to see if it is straight. Check periodically.
Make a straightening tear when necessary.

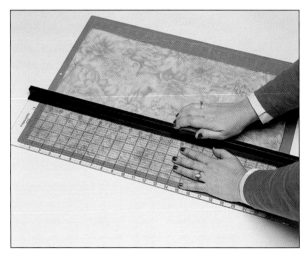

A ruler/cutter combination tool can also be used for cutting strips.

Cutting Squares and Rectangles

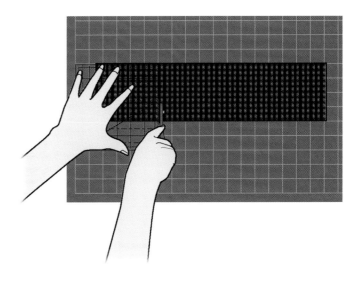

1. Cut designated size strips. Layer several on cutting mat.

2. Square off left end. Cut squares or rectangles smaller than 6" with 6" Square Up ruler. Cut squares larger than 6" with 12½" Square Up.

Sewing Suggestions

- Use a fine sharp, #80/12 needle.
- Use a neutral color thread as white, beige, or gray. Dark thread for sewing parts of the blocks may be preferred so that stitching does not show.
- Use small stitches, approximately 15 per inch.
- Use the same sewing machine throughout your quilt.
- Do not backstitch, except where indicated.
- Complete the ¼" Seam Allowance Test before starting.

¼" Seam Allowance

Use a consistent seam allowance throughout the construction of the quilt. If necessary, adjust the needle position, change the presser foot, or feed the fabric under the presser foot to achieve the ¼".

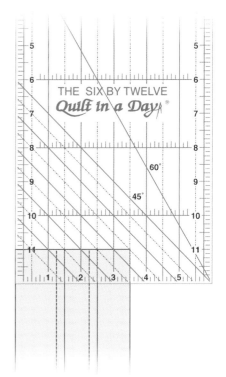

The ¼" Seam Allowance Test

1. Using the rotary cutter and ruler, accurately cut a 1½" strip of background fabric.

2. Cut off (3) 1½" x 6" pieces from the strip.

3. Sew the three strips together lengthwise with what you think is a ¼" seam.

4. Press the seams in one direction. Make sure no folds occur at the seam when pressing.

5. Place the sewn sample under a ruler and measure its width. It should measure exactly 3½" wide. If sample measures smaller than 3½", seam is too large. If sample measures larger than 3½", seam is too small.

6. Adjust the seam allowance and repeat if necessary.

Pressing and Applique

Stiletto

Use the stiletto to separate pieces of fabric, feed patches through the sewing machine, and hold seams flat as you stitch over them. The stiletto can also be used to remove unwanted stitches.

Pressing

Use a gridded pressing mat to line up and press pieces straight. The cushion allows seams to "sink in" so the piece can be pressed flat.

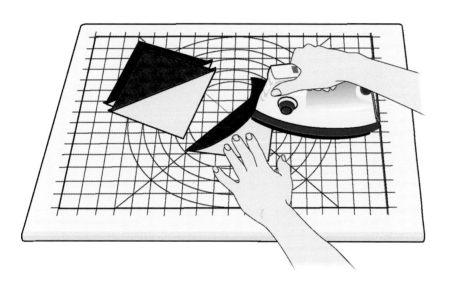

1. Lay pieces on the pressing mat with the darker fabric on top.

2. Open and press the seam allowance to the darker fabric, unless you are directed otherwise for easier construction as in the Flying Geese and Tree blocks.

3. Press carefully to avoid leaving folds at seam lines. Using steam is a personal preference.

Applique using Paper Backed Fusible Interfacing

1. Place paper backed fusible interfacing on top of pattern, paper side up.

2. Trace the patterns on the paper side of the fusible interfacing.

3. Roughly cut around the shape. Place on the wrong side of the fabric to be appliqued. Make sure the fabric is larger than the paper.

4. Following manufacturer's directions, press the paper backed fusible interfacing to the fabric.

5. Cut out around the shape, and peel away the paper. Be careful to leave the thin web of fusing attached to the fabric.

6. Position the applique with fabric right side up. Press in place.

7. Stitch around the outside edge with a zig-zag or blanket stitch, using invisible or matching thread.

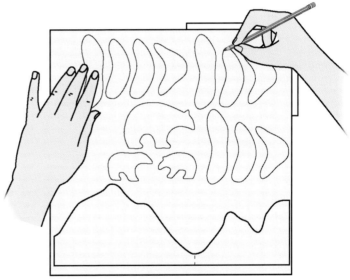

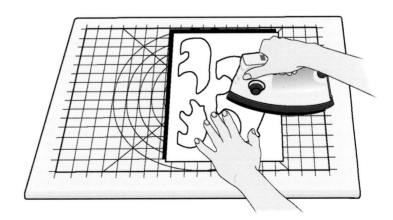

Practice Blocks

Before you begin making all the blocks for the Bears in the Woods quilt, it is best to make one sample of each block. The sewing technique is the same as in the regular instructions. This is to ensure you understand the process and that you are using a good ¼" seam allowance. All four blocks must end up the same size. All measurements given in inches and are for cutting purposes.

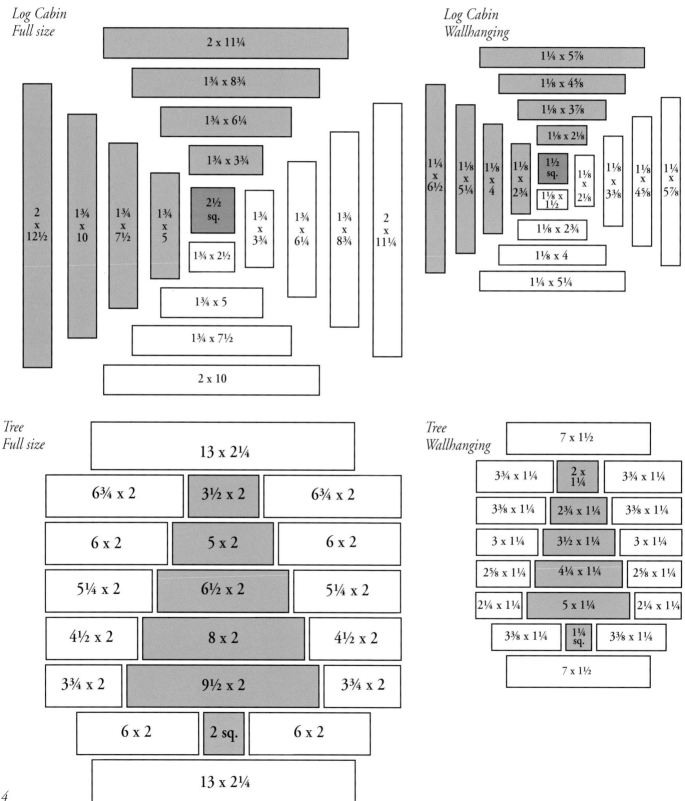

Log Cabin Full size

2 x 11¼
1¾ x 8¾
1¾ x 6¼
1¾ x 3¾
2½ sq.
1¾ x 2½
1¾ x 5
1¾ x 7½
2 x 10
2 x 12½
1¾ x 10
1¾ x 7½
1¾ x 5
1¾ x 3¾
1¾ x 6¼
1¾ x 8¾
2 x 11¼

Log Cabin Wallhanging

1¼ x 5⅞
1⅛ x 4⅝
1⅛ x 3⅞
1⅛ x 2⅛
1½ sq.
1⅛ x 1½
1⅛ x 2¾
1⅛ x 4
1¼ x 5¼
1¼ x 6½
1⅛ x 5¼
1⅛ x 4
1⅛ x 2¾
1⅛ x 2⅛
1⅛ x 3⅜
1⅛ x 4⅝
1¼ x 5⅞

Tree Full size

13 x 2¼
6¾ x 2 | 3½ x 2 | 6¾ x 2
6 x 2 | 5 x 2 | 6 x 2
5¼ x 2 | 6½ x 2 | 5¼ x 2
4½ x 2 | 8 x 2 | 4½ x 2
3¾ x 2 | 9½ x 2 | 3¾ x 2
6 x 2 | 2 sq. | 6 x 2
13 x 2¼

Tree Wallhanging

7 x 1½
3¾ x 1¼ | 2 x 1¼ | 3¾ x 1¼
3⅜ x 1¼ | 2¾ x 1¼ | 3⅜ x 1¼
3 x 1¼ | 3½ x 1¼ | 3 x 1¼
2⅝ x 1¼ | 4¼ x 1¼ | 2⅝ x 1¼
2¼ x 1¼ | 5 x 1¼ | 2¼ x 1¼
3⅜ x 1¼ | 1¼ sq. | 3⅜ x 1¼
7 x 1½

Practice Blocks

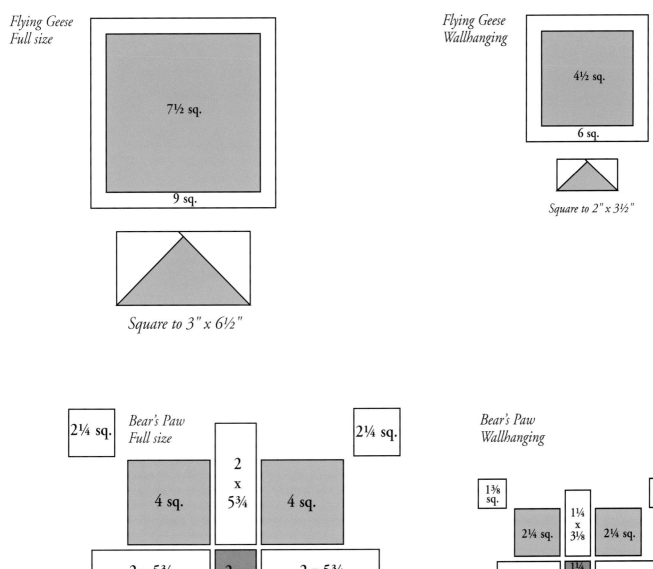

*Flying Geese
Full size*

7½ sq.

9 sq.

Square to 3" x 6½"

*Flying Geese
Wallhanging*

4½ sq.

6 sq.

Square to 2" x 3½"

*Bear's Paw
Full size*

2¼ sq.

2¼ sq.

4 sq.

2
x
5¾

4 sq.

2 x 5¾

2 sq.

2 x 5¾

4 sq.

2
x
5¾

4 sq.

2¼ sq.

2¼ sq.

*Grid for
Claws 6" x
12" each
Square to
2¼" square*

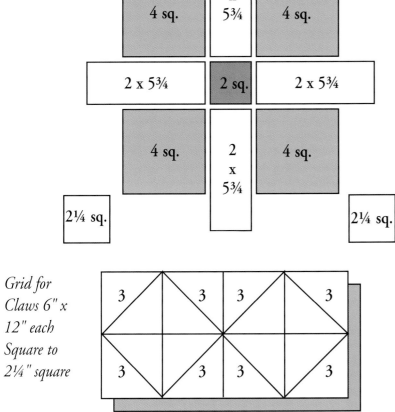

3 3 3 3

3 3 3 3

*Bear's Paw
Wallhanging*

1⅜ sq.

1⅜ sq.

2¼ sq.

1¼
x
3⅛

2¼ sq.

1¼ x 3⅛

1¼ sq.

1¼ x 3⅛

2¼ sq.

1¼
x
3⅛

2¼ sq.

1⅜ sq.

1⅜ sq.

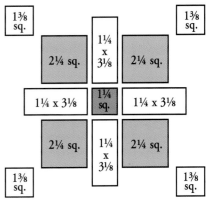

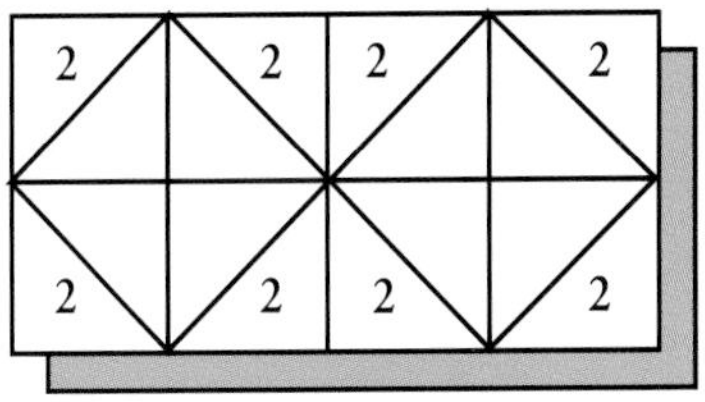

2 2 2 2

2 2 2 2

*Grid for Claws
4" x 8" each
Square to 1⅜" square*

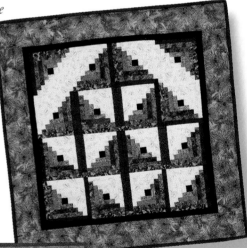

the Log Cabin

Linda Dallman
Forest Home

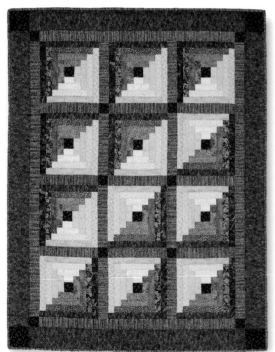

Sue Bouchard
Timber Line

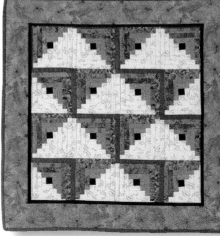

Linda Dallman
Trees

16

Yardage and Cutting for Twelve Log Cabin Blocks

This is a repeat of the yardage on page 9.

	Full Size 12" Finished Block	Wallhanging 6" Finished Block
Background Fabric	1⅓ yds	¾ yd
B1	(4) 1¾" strips	(2) 1⅛" strips
B2	(5) 1¾" strips	(2) 1⅛" strips
B3	(6) 1¾" strips	(4) 1⅛" strips
B4	*(8) 2" strips	*(4) 1⅜" strips
Center Square	⅛ yd (1) 2½" strip	⅛ yd (1) 1½" strip
First Dark Second Dark Third Dark	⅛ yd of each (2) 1¾" strips from each	⅛ yd of each (1) 1⅛" strip from each
Fourth Dark Fifth Dark Sixth Dark	¼ yd of each (3) 1¾" strips from each	⅛ yd of each (2) 1⅛" strips from each
Seventh Dark Eighth Dark	⅓ yd of each *(4) 2" strips from each	⅛ yd of each *(2) 1⅜" strips from each

Blocks in the Bears in the Woods quilt must all finish the same size to fit together. The Log Cabin blocks tend to measure smaller because of all the seams. The B4, Seventh Dark, and Eighth Dark strips are ¼" wider than the other strips to compensate for a possible "smaller" block. Completed blocks are squared to 12½" and 6½".

Tablerunner
Teresa Varnes

Paste-Up Page

Paste in your fabric swatches. Center is used only once. Background is used twice each round. Each Dark is used only once.

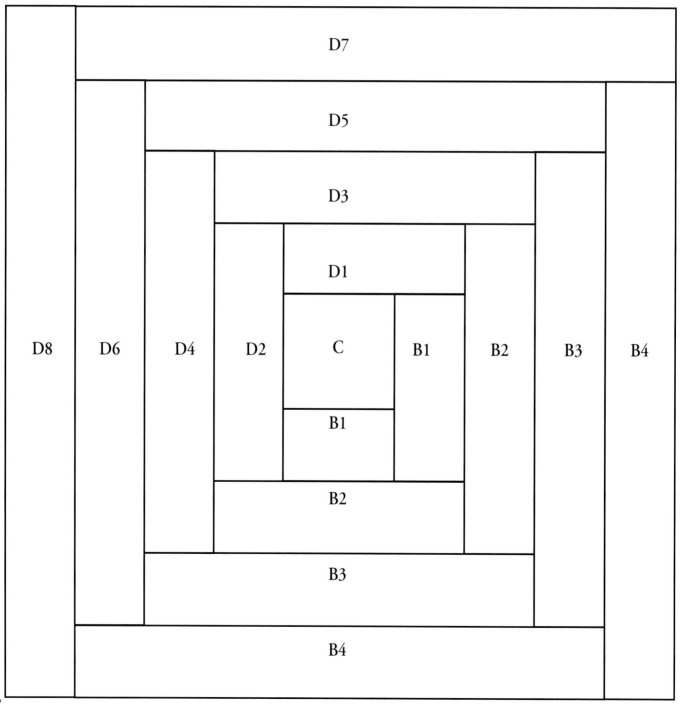

Log Cabin

Making the Blocks

Arranging the Strips

1. Place the strips to the right of your sewing machine in sewing order.

   Background strips alternate with two dark strips.

   Background strips are referred to as B strips. (B❶ through❹)

   Dark strips are referred to as D strips. (D❶ through D❽)

Center

Background B1

First Dark D1

Second Dark D2

Background B2

Third Dark D3

Fourth Dark D4

Background B3

Fifth Dark D5

Sixth Dark D6

Background B4

Seventh Dark D7

Eighth Dark D8

Making the Center Squares

1. Place Background strip B❶ right sides together to Center strip.

2. Sew the two strips together lengthwise, with B❶ on the top.

   Use a ¼" seam allowance Sew with 15 stitches per inch, or a #2 stitch setting.

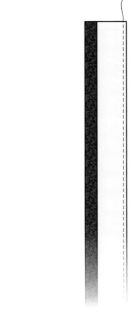

C   B❶

3. Lay sewn strips on a cutting mat. Square off the left end, removing the selvages.

4. Cut into segments using the 6" x 6" ruler and rotary cutter.

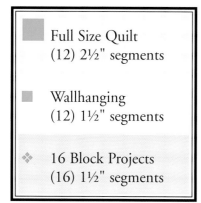

Full Size Quilt
(12) 2½" segments

Wallhanging
(12) 1½" segments

❖ 16 Block Projects
(16) 1½" segments

5. Stack.

6. Center fabric is used only once in the block. Remove Center left-overs from area.

- **Background strips are used twice each round.**

- **Darks are each used only once.**

Finger Pressing

It is best not to press Log Cabin blocks with iron after each step of construction, as ironing distorts blocks. However, seams should be directed and finger pressed open.

1. Turn stack.

2. Lift up Background B❶ strip, or the strip you just added.

3. Finger press and crease seam flat. **Always press seam away from Center square.**

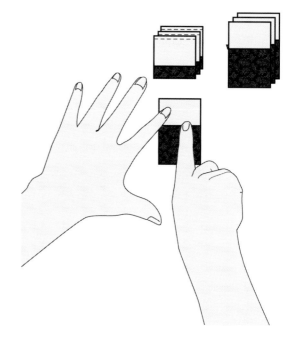

Adding Another Background B❶ Strip

1. Place stack so B❶ is on top, wrong side up.

2. Place a second Background B❶ strip right side up under the presser foot. Stitch an inch to hold the strip in place.

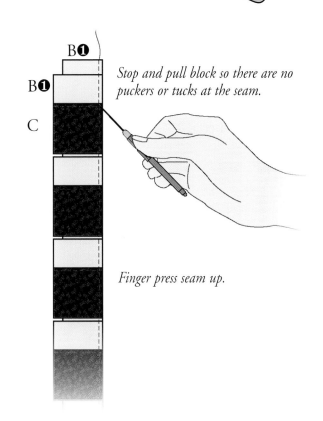

3. Place a block right sides together to the strip with B❶ at the top.

4. Anchor with an inch of stitching.

5. Sew, finger pressing the seam allowance up toward Background B❶. Use the stiletto to hold the seam flat.

6. As you near the end of the block, pick up the second block.

7. Butt it after the first block.

8. Sew all blocks, always placing Background B❶ toward the top, and pressing the seam allowance up.

9. When there is not enough strip for an additional block, start a new strip.

B❶

B❶

C

Stop and pull block so there are no puckers or tucks at the seam.

Finger press seam up.

10. Lay strips on cutting mat along a grid line.

11. Line up a 6" x 6" ruler with the outside edge, and cut between blocks. Trim if necessary.

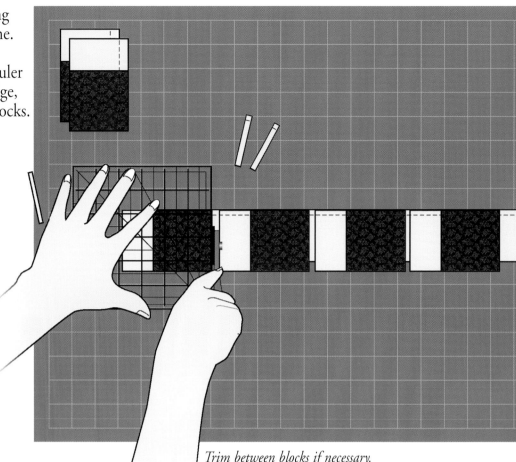

Trim between blocks if necessary.
Cut straight edges.

12. Stack. Turn stack over.

13. Open the Background B❶ strip, and finger press seam.

14. Open and check block against your Paste-Up page.

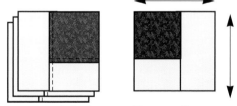

Measure and check your ¼" seam allowance.

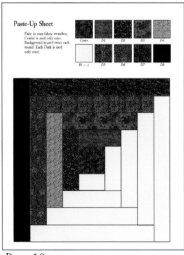

Page 18

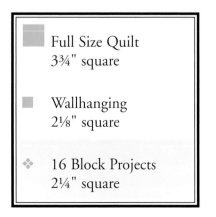

Full Size Quilt
3¾" square

Wallhanging
2⅛" square

❖   16 Block Projects
2¼" square

Adding the First Dark D❶ Strip

1. Place a D❶ strip under presser foot, right side up.

2. Place block right sides together to strip, with B❶ strip across the top.

3. Sew the length of the block, finger pressing the seam up and flat.

4. Butt and sew on next blocks, until a D❶ strip has been added to all blocks. Start a new strip as needed.

5. Lay strip on cutting mat, with blocks on top.

6. Cut apart between blocks. Stack. Turn over.

7. Open and finger press last strip seam.

8. Remove extra D❶ strip from area.

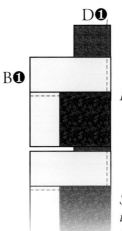

Finger press seam up.

Stop and pull block so there are no puckers or tucks at the seam.

Adding the Second Dark D❷ Strip

1. Place a D❷ strip under presser foot, right side up.

2. Place block with D❶ strip across top and perpendicular to D❷ strip.

3. Sew the length of the block, pushing the first seam up and flat, and the second seam down and flat.

   As the block construction progresses, there will be these two seams. Always push the first seam up and flat, and second seam down and flat.

4. Continue butting and sewing blocks, until D❷ strip is added to all blocks.

5. Cut apart between blocks. Stack. Turn stack over.

6. Open and finger press last strip seam.

7. Remove extra D❷ strips from sewing area.

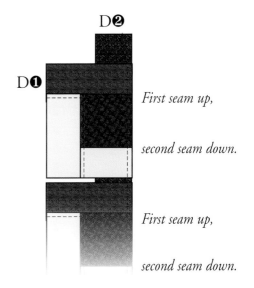

First seam up,

second seam down.

First seam up,

second seam down.

Adding Background B❷ Strips

1. Place a B❷ strip under presser foot, right side up.

2. Place block with Second Dark D❷ strip across top and perpendicular to the new strip.

3. Sew all blocks, pushing first seams up and second seams down. The wrong side of the block lies flat from the Center out.

4. Cut apart. Stack. Turn over.

5. Open and finger press last strip seam.

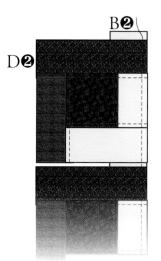

Seams lie flat from the center out.

6. Place a second B❷ strip under presser foot.

7. Place block with first B❷ strip across top and perpendicular to new strip.

8. Sew all blocks.

9. Cut apart. Stack. Turn stack over.

10. Open and finger press last strip seam.

11. Remove extra B❷ strips from sewing area.

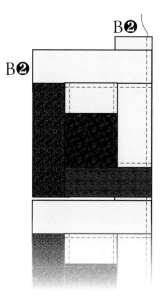

Adding Dark D❸ and D❹ Strips

1. Place a D❸ strip under presser foot, right side up.

2. Place block with second B❷ strip across top and perpendicular to new strip.

3. Sew all blocks.

4. Cut apart. Stack. Turn stack over.

5. Open and finger press last strip seam.

6. Remove extra D❸ strips from sewing area.

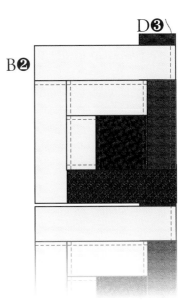

7. Place a D❹ strip under presser foot.

8. Place block with D❸ across top.

9. Sew all blocks.

10. Cut apart. Stack. Turn stack over.

11. Open and finger press last strip seam.

12. Remove extra D❹ strips from sewing area.

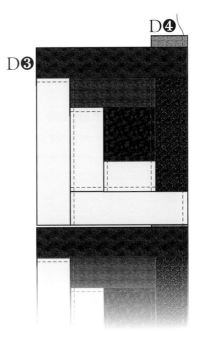

Adding Background B❸ Strips

1. Place a B❸ strip under presser foot.

2. Place block with D❹ across top.

3. Sew all blocks.

4. Cut apart. Stack. Turn stack over.

5. Open and finger press last strip seam.

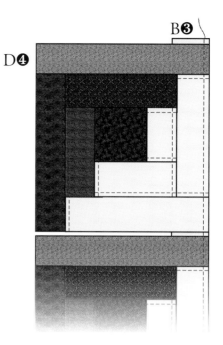

6. Place another B❸ strip under presser foot.

7. Place block with B❸ across top.

8. Sew all blocks.

9. Cut apart. Stack. Turn stack over.

10. Open and finger press last strip seam.

11. Remove extra B❸ strips from sewing area.

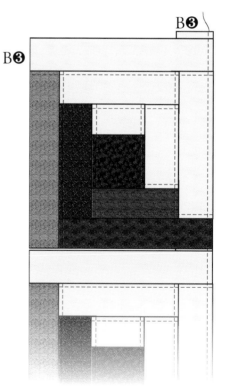

Adding Dark D**❺** and D**❻** Strips

1. Place a D**❺** strip under presser foot.

2. Place block with B**❸** strip across top and perpendicular to new strip.

3. Sew all blocks.

4. Cut apart. Stack. Turn stack over.

5. Open and finger press last strip seam.

6. Remove extra D**❺** strips from area.

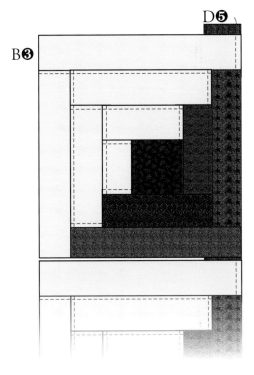

7. Place a D**❻** strip under presser foot.

8. Place block with D**❺** across top.

9. Sew all blocks.

10. Cut apart. Stack. Turn stack over.

11. Open and finger press last strip seam.

12. Remove extra D**❻** strips from sewing area.

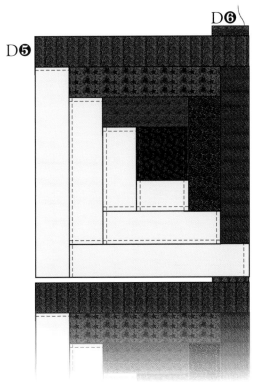

Adding Background B❹ Strips

1. Place a B❹ strip under presser foot.

2. Place block with D❻ across top.

3. Sew all blocks.

4. Cut apart. Stack. Turn stack over.

5. Open and finger press last strip seam.

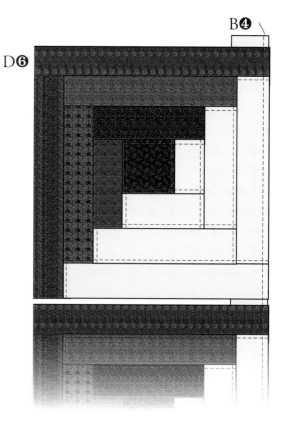

6. Place another B❹ strip under presser foot.

7. Place block with B❹ across top.

8. Sew all blocks.

9. Cut apart. Stack. Turn stack over.

10. Open and finger press last strip seam.

11. Remove extra B❹ strips from sewing area.

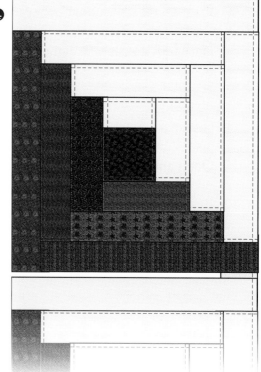

Adding Dark D❼ and D❽ Strips

1. Place a D❼ strip under presser foot.

2. Place block with B❹ across top.

3. Sew all blocks.

4. Cut apart. Stack. Turn stack over.

5. Open and finger press last strip seam.

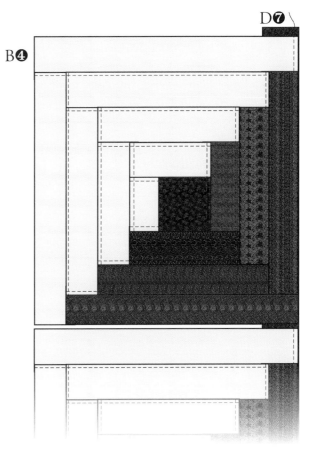

6. Place a D❽ strip under presser foot.

7. Place block with D❼ across top.

8. Sew all blocks.

9. Cut apart. Stack. Turn stack over.

10. Open and finger press last strip seam.

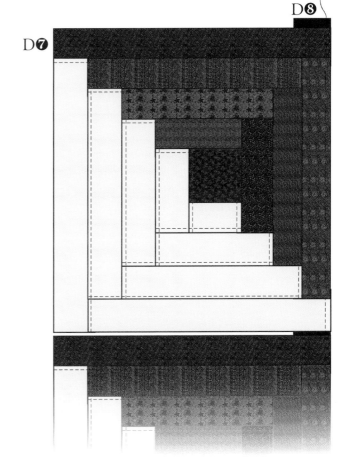

Pressing the Block

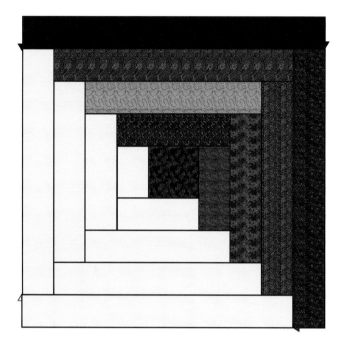

1. Press each block from the right side.

2. Press from the wrong side, making sure there are no tucks at the seams.

3. Blocks are squared to this size, so they fit with other blocks.

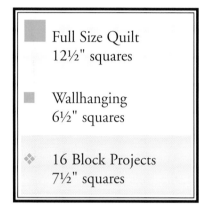

Full Size Quilt
12½" squares

Wallhanging
6½" squares

❖ 16 Block Projects
7½" squares

4. Re-press blocks that are smaller than desired size.

5. Sliver trim blocks equally on four sides to designated size.

- **Place the diagonal line of the 12½" ruler across the center of the block.**

- **Trim on two sides.**

- **Turn, and trim equal amounts on the remaining two sides.**

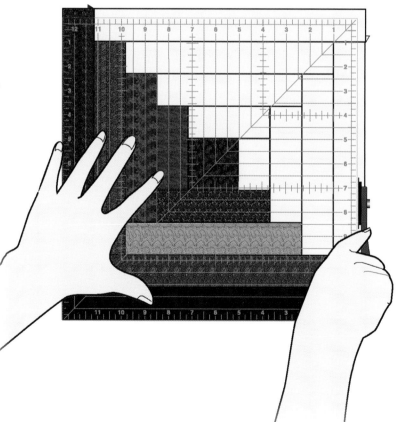

The Log Cabin pattern is one of America's best loved patterns, and has remained popular through the ages. Many believe it first originated to honor our beloved president, Abraham Lincoln. Quiltmakers began with a traditional red center to represent the hearth, or chimney. The light side of the block represents the sun in front of the cabin, and the dark side is the shadow behind the cabin. However, historians have actually traced the pattern back 2,700 years to log cabin wrappings on Egyptian mummies.

1930's blocks

Wool quilt from the late 1800's

Victorian block

Base fabric

The thirty block log cabin in the barn raising layout was made in the late 1800's from wool with a foundation piecing method. The quiltmaker began with a scrap piece of base fabric, and starting with the center, stitched the strips through the base in counter clockwise order.

In the Victorian era, when many were making Crazy Quilts, this quiltmaker pieced her logs from strips of ribbon, and then embellished them with hand decorative stitches.

The bright orange center accents these log cabin blocks made in the 1930's. A light and dark side clearly show, even in these scrappy fabrics.

31

Timber Line

Yardage and Cutting Chart for 12 Block Log Cabin

In addition to the yardage requirements for 12 full size blocks on page 17, you need the following fabrics to finish this quilt.

Lattice
1 yd
(6) 2½" strips into
(17) 2½" x 12½"
(5) 2½" strips

Cornerstones
⅛ yd
(10) 2½" x 2½"

Border
¾ yd
(5) 4½" strips

Border Corners
¼ yd
(4) 4½" x 4½"

Binding
⅝ yd
(6) 3" strips

Batting
59" x 59"

Backing
3½ yds

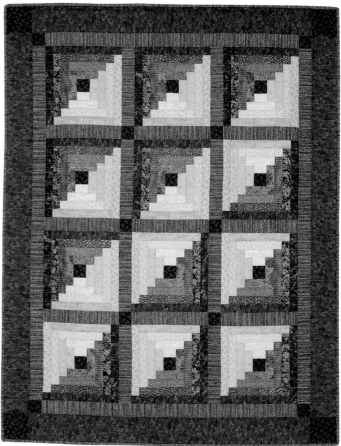

Approximate Finished Size 52½" x 64½"
Sue Bouchard

1. Make twelve Log Cabin blocks.

2. Lay out the twelve blocks with seventeen lattice and six cornerstones.

3. Flip second vertical row onto first. Stack from bottom to top, so first block is on top. Assembly-line sew. Do not clip connecting threads.

4. Stack third row from bottom to top, and assembly-line sew to first two vertical rows.

5. Sew remaining vertical rows. Press seams toward lattice.

6. Sew horizontal rows.

7. Sew three 2½" strips together into one long strip. Measure sides, and cut two strips.

8. Measure and cut two strips for top and bottom.

9. Pin and sew on sides.

10. Add 2½" cornerstones to top and bottom strips. Pin and sew to quilt top.

11. Sew five 4½" border strips together. Repeat process.

Mantle Cover

Original Design by Diane Kleinhans
Sewn by Teresa Varnes

The Mantel Cover is made from finished size 6" Log Cabin and 1½" x 3" Flying Geese patches. Use these calculations to customize a cover for your mantle.

1. Measure your mantle, or the area you wish to cover.

2. Figure out how many Log Cabin blocks you need to make by dividing your length by 8½", the measurement across the diagonal of a Log Cabin block minus seam allowance. Round down to a whole number.

3. Make the necessary number of Log Cabin blocks. See pages 17-30 for the Wallhanging size blocks.

4. Cut 10" Background squares into fourths on both diagonals. Cut one 5½" Background square in half on one diagonal.

5. Sew Log Cabin blocks together with Background triangles.

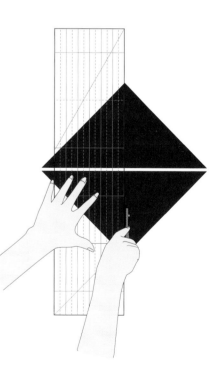

6. Figure out how many Flying Geese patches you need to make by measuring the sewn together top, and dividing by 1½", the finished width of a Geese block.

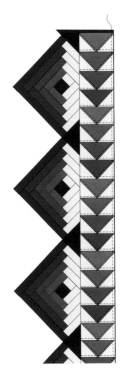

7. Make the Geese patches. See pages 95-98 for the Wallhanging size patches.

8. Sew Geese together into one long strip, see page 120, and sew to Log Cabin blocks.

9. Measure the depth of the mantle, and cut a piece of fabric that depth plus ½" seam allowance, by length of sewn together top. Cut piece, and add.

10. Place top right sides together to backing. Sew around outside edge, leaving an opening for turning. Trim. Turn right side out. Whipstitch opening shut.

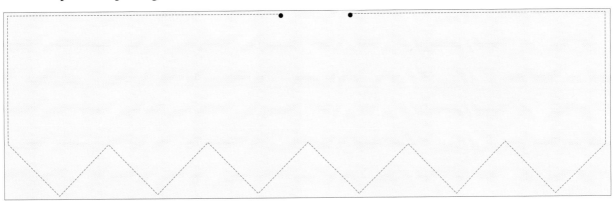

11. Embellish with purchased tassels.

Sixteen Block Projects

Christmas Tablerunner
Approximate Finished Size 20" x 62"
Pat Wetzel

Trees
Approximate Finished Size 34" x 34"
Linda Dallman

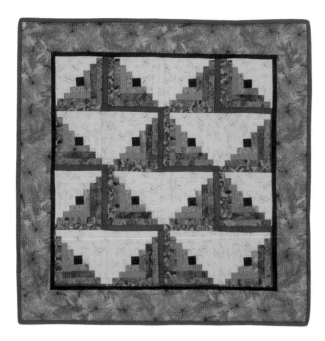

Star
Approximate Finished Size 34" x 34"
Pat Wetzel

Forest Home
Approximate Finished Size 34" x 34"
Linda Dallman

Yardage and Cutting Chart for 16 Blocks

7" Finished Block

Background	¾ yd	B1 (2) 1¼" strips
		B2 (4) 1¼" strips
		B3 (5) 1¼" strips
		B4 (6) 1½" strips
Center Square	⅛ yd	(1) 1½" strip
First Dark	⅛ yd of each	(1) 1¼" strip
Second Dark		(2) 1¼" strips
Third Dark		(2) 1¼" strips
Fourth Dark		(2) 1¼" strips
Fifth Dark	¼ yd of each	(3) 1¼" strips
Sixth Dark		(3) 1¼" strips
Seventh Dark		(3) 1½" strips
Eighth Dark	¼ yd	(4) 1½" strips
Folded Border	¼ yd	(4) 1¼" strips
Border	½ yd	(4) 3½" strips
Binding	½ yd	(4) 3" strips

Wallhanging Backing and Batting - 36" square
Tablerunner Backing and Batting - 24" x 66"

Making Your Top

1. Make 16 blocks following the instructions on pages 19-30.

2. Lay out in your selected pattern.

3. Sew blocks together.

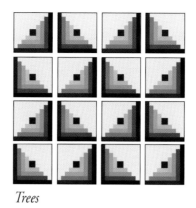

Trees

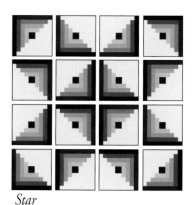

Star

Tablerunner

Finishing

1. Press 1¼" Folded Border strips in half lengthwise, **wrong sides** together.

2. Cut two strips the measurement of the two sides.

3. Match and pin raw edges of quilt and Folded Border. Sew with a **scant** ¼" seam and a long stitch, or 6-8 stitches per inch. Set seams. Do not fold out.

4. Cut two strips the measurement of top and bottom.

5. Pin and sew to quilt. Do not fold out. Set seams.

6. Add 3½" borders.

7. Machine quilt and bind. See page 122.

Forest Home

1. Make sixteen **partial** log cabin blocks following the instructions on pages 19-30. Stop after adding Dark D❻.

2. Divide the blocks into two groups of eight.

3. Finish the first group of eight as instructed on pages 28-30.

4. Lay out eight partial blocks in two stacks with four in each stack.

5. Sew a B❹ strip to eight blocks. Place back in two stacks.

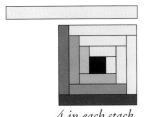 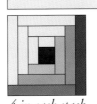

4 in each stack   *4 in each stack*

6. Sew a Trunk strip to each block.

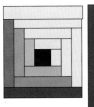 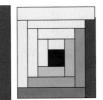

7. Sew D❼ and D❽ to each block.

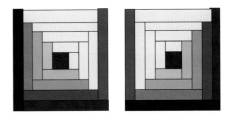

8. Sew the top together.

9. Add borders and finish. See pages 122-128.

the Tree Block

Caribou Crossing
Sue Bouchard

Tree Skirt
Teresa Varnes

Twelve Block Tree
Sue Bouchard

Yardage and Cutting Chart for Twenty Trees

This is a repeat of the yardage on page 9.

	Full Size 12" Finished Block	Wallhanging 6" Finished Block
Ten Different Greens	¼ yd of each (2) 2" strips from each	⅛ yd of each (2) 1¼" strips from each
Two Trunks	⅛ yd of each (1) 2" strip from each	⅛ yd of each (1) 1¼" strip from each
Background	3 yds (2) 6" strips (14) 2¼" strips (27) 2" strips	1⅛ yds (2) 3⅜" strips (8) 1½" strips (17) 1¼" strips

Cutting the Tree Rows

There are five different green fabrics in each Tree.

1. Open five different strips of greens. Press center folds flat. Layer selvage to selvage, right side up. Stack on cutting mat.

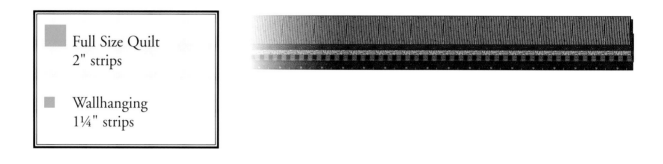

Full Size Quilt
2" strips

Wallhanging
1¼" strips

2. Using a rotary cutter, remove selvages from left end.

3. Cut five segments from largest to smallest.

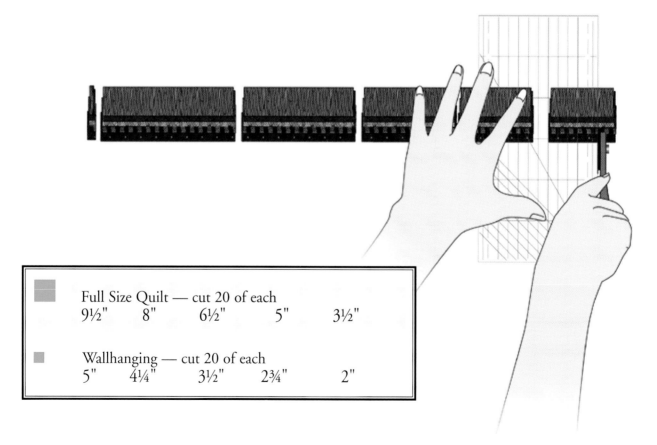

Full Size Quilt — cut 20 of each
9½"   8"   6½"   5"   3½"

Wallhanging — cut 20 of each
5"   4¼"   3½"   2¾"   2"

Full Size Quilt

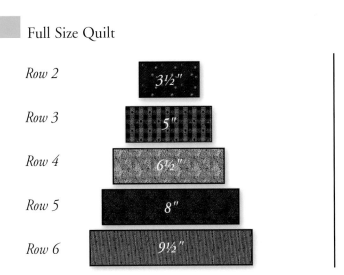

Row 2 3½"
Row 3 5"
Row 4 6½"
Row 5 8"
Row 6 9½"

Wallhanging

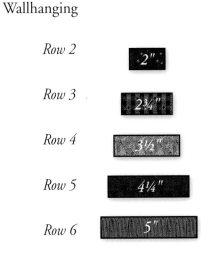

Row 2 2"
Row 3 2¾"
Row 4 3½"
Row 5 4¼"
Row 6 5"

4. Place stacks in Tree layout as you cut.

5. Repeat until you have 20 pieces in each stack.

Cutting the Background Fabric

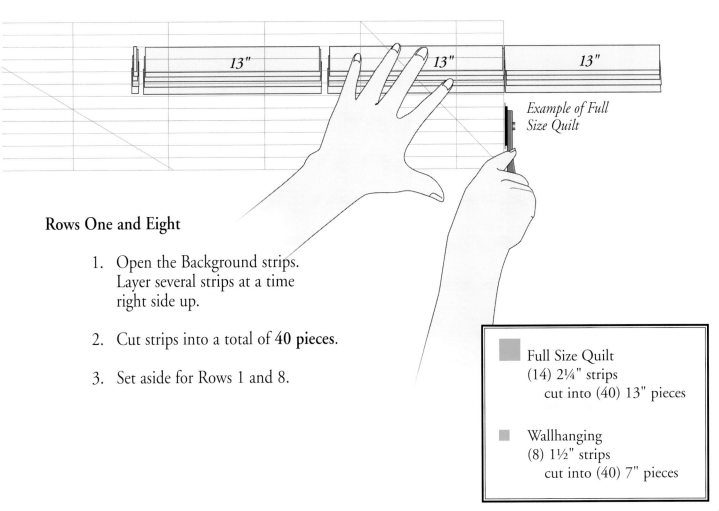

13"   13"   13"

Example of Full Size Quilt

Rows One and Eight

1. Open the Background strips. Layer several strips at a time right side up.

2. Cut strips into a total of **40 pieces**.

3. Set aside for Rows 1 and 8.

Full Size Quilt
(14) 2¼" strips
   cut into (40) 13" pieces

Wallhanging
(8) 1½" strips
   cut into (40) 7" pieces

43

Rows Two through Six

1. Count out Background strips.

2. Open and layer **right side up** according to the number needed for each designated row.

3. Cut into specified lengths until **40 pieces** are cut for each row.

4. Lay out all the pieces required to complete Rows Two through Six.

Make two stacks with twenty in each stack.

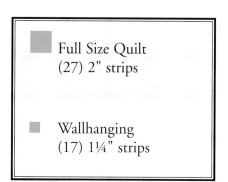

Full Size Quilt	(27) 2" strips
Wallhanging	(17) 1¼" strips

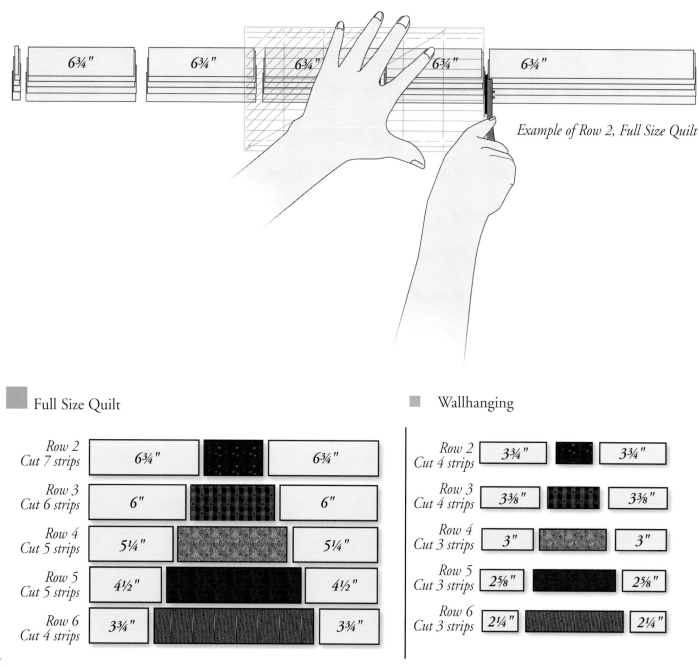

Example of Row 2, Full Size Quilt

Full Size Quilt

Row 2 Cut 7 strips	6¾"		6¾"
Row 3 Cut 6 strips	6"		6"
Row 4 Cut 5 strips	5¼"		5¼"
Row 5 Cut 5 strips	4½"		4½"
Row 6 Cut 4 strips	3¾"		3¾"

Wallhanging

Row 2 Cut 4 strips	3¾"		3¾"
Row 3 Cut 4 strips	3⅜"		3⅜"
Row 4 Cut 3 strips	3"		3"
Row 5 Cut 3 strips	2⅝"		2⅝"
Row 6 Cut 3 strips	2¼"		2¼"

Assembly-line Marking Diagonal Lines

1. Turn Background strips wrong side up.

2. Place two strips from same row on gridded cutting mat. Line up on grid.

3. Place the 6" Square Up ruler's 45º line on the center point.

4. With a soft, sharp pencil, draw diagonal lines.

5. Make two stacks for each row.

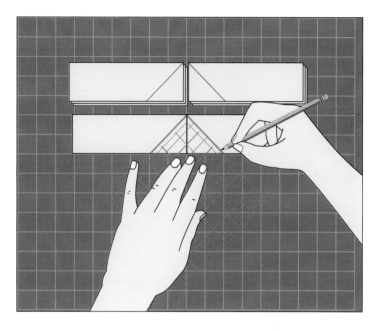

6. Turn rows around.

7. Place Background strips back in Tree layout **wrong side up** in this order, so rows are ready for sewing.

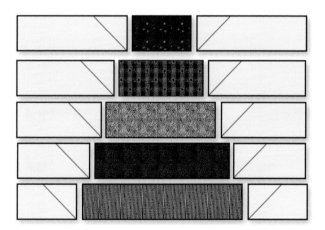

Diagonal Line Sewing

1. Center your needle.

2. Place a multi-purpose foot, marked with a center groove, on your machine.

3. Line up the groove on the diagonal line as you sew.

Sewing Row Two Together

1. Separate out Row 2.

2. Place right Background strip on Tree strip, right sides together. Line up the top and side edges evenly.

3. *Optional:* Pin in place. Do not pin across diagonally drawn line.

Full Size Quilt

Wallhanging

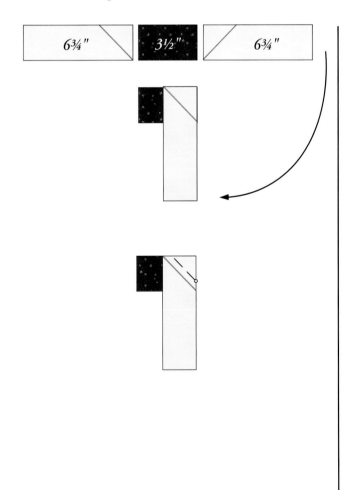

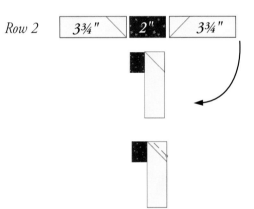

4. Assembly-line sew **on drawn lines**. Pull the threads
    to get the strip started. Use stiletto to help feed strips
    through sewing machine.

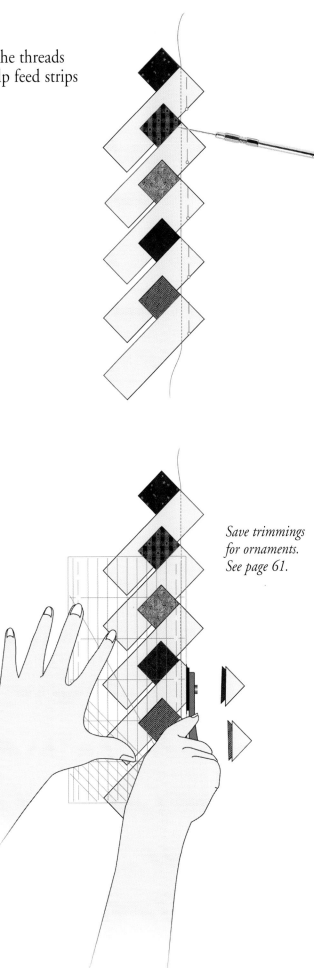

5. Clip apart in groups of five.

6. Place ¼" line on 6" x 12"
    ruler on stitching line. Trim
    seam allowances to ¼".

7. Set seams. Open and press
    seam allowances toward
    Background fabric.
    Clip apart.

*Save trimmings
for ornaments.
See page 61.*

Sewing the Left Side of Tree

1. Turn the Tree upside down. Place the Background strip on the Tree.

2. *Optional:* Pin in place.

3. Assembly-line sew on drawn line.

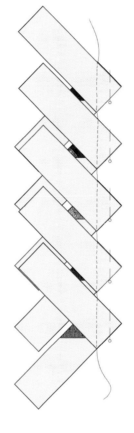

4. Trim seam allowances to ¼".

5. Set seams. Open and press seam allowances toward Background fabric.

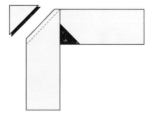

6. Fold in half and crease.

Rows 3 through 6

Repeat pinning, sewing, trimming and pressing process for the remaining Tree rows.

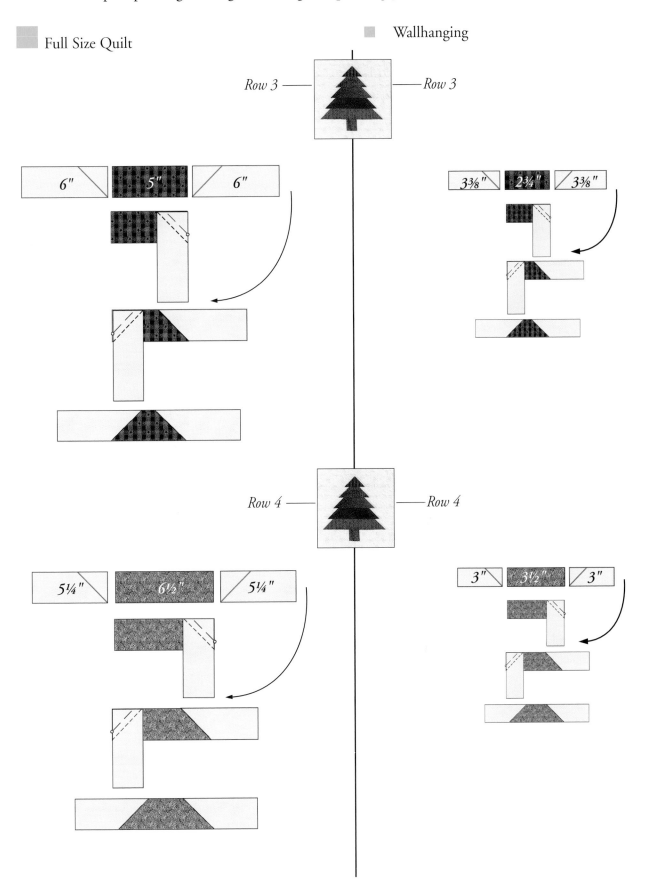

Wallhanging

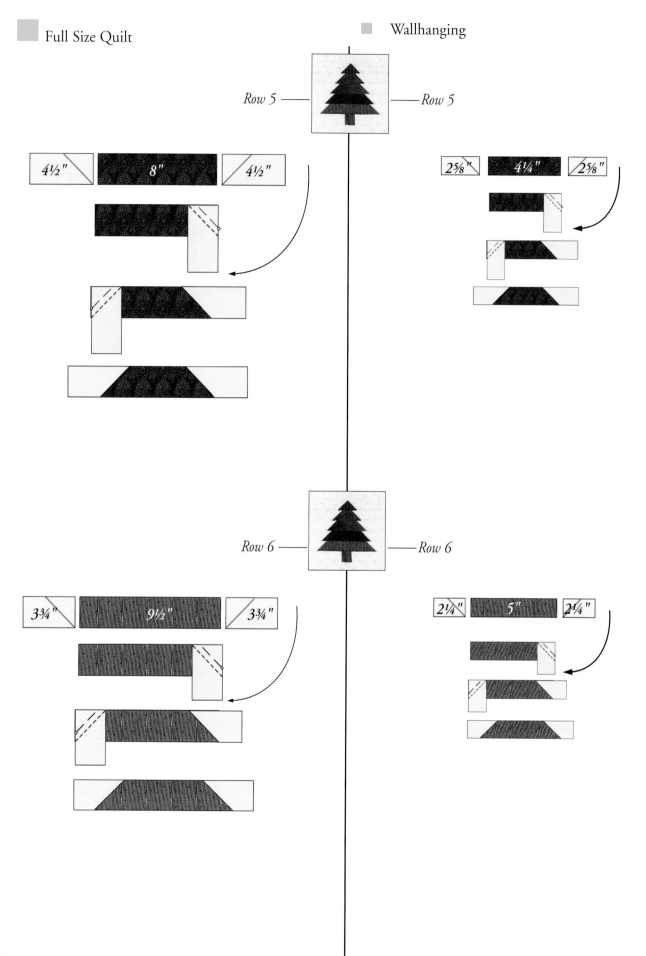

Row 5 — — Row 5

4½"   8"   4½"

2⅝"   4¼"   2⅝"

Row 6 — — Row 6

3¾"   9½"   3¾"

2¼"   5"   2¼"

Making Trunk Row 7

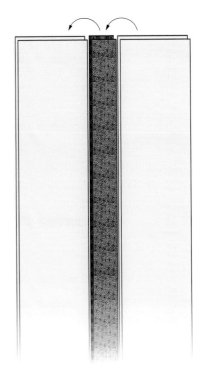

1. Cut two Background strips in half and two Trunk strips in half. Discard one half of each Trunk strip.

2. Lay out a Background half strip on both sides of the Trunk half strips.

> ▮ **Full Size Quilt**
> 6" Background strips
> 2" Trunk strips
>
> ▮ **Wallhanging**
> 3⅜" Background strips
> 1¼" Trunk strips

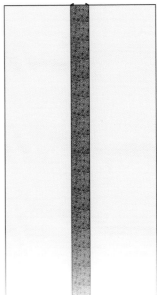

3. Sew with a ¼" seam and 15 stitches per inch.

4. Press seam allowances toward the Trunk fabric.

5. Lay Trunk Row on cutting mat, lining up the edge of the fabric on a line of the mat. Square left edge.

6. Cut each strip set into (10) segments.

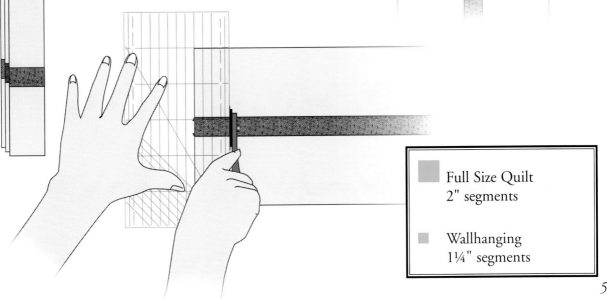

> ▮ **Full Size Quilt**
> 2" segments
>
> ▮ **Wallhanging**
> 1¼" segments

Completing the Tree Block

1. Sort Trunk rows into two stacks of ten according to Trunk color.

2. In each stack lay out rows for one Tree block in the same color. Include strips for Rows 1 and 8.

3. Continue to stack matching Trees until you have ten different blocks in each stack.

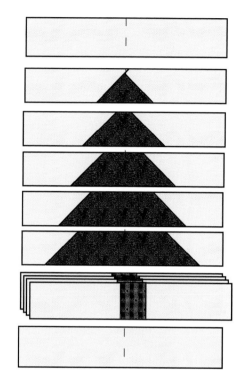 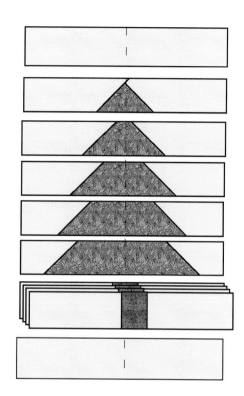

4. Mix up Tree strips by rows.

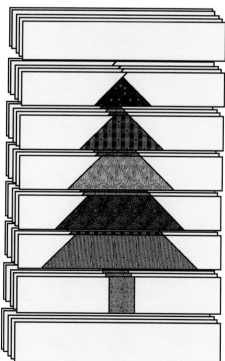

Leave in original order.

Take last piece and move to top.

Take last two pieces and move to top.

Take last three pieces and move to top.

Take last four pieces and move to top.

5. Flip Row 2 right sides together to Row 1.
   Flip Row 4 to Row 3.
   Flip Row 6 to Row 5.
   Flip Row 8 to Row 7.

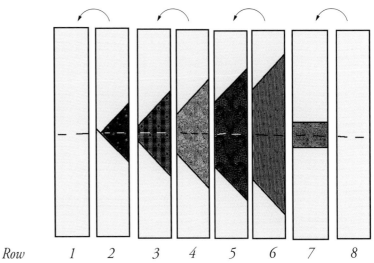

Row   1   2   3   4   5   6   7   8

6. Match the center creases. Assembly-line
   sew Row 2 to Row 1. Hold down seams
   with stiletto.

7. Assembly-line sew Row 4 to
   Row 3, Row 6 to Row 5 and
   Row 8 to Row 7.

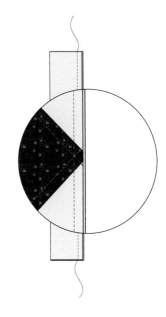

8. Assembly-line sew
   Row 3/4 to Row 1/2 and
   Row 7/8 to Row 5/6.

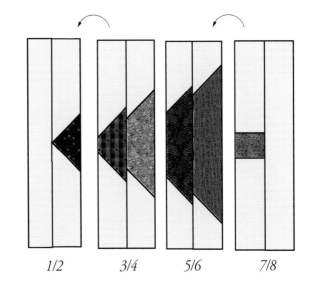

Row   1/2   3/4   5/6   7/8

9. Assembly-line sew the top half of the Tree to the bottom half. Do not press.

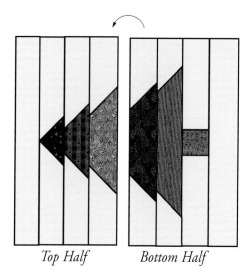

Top Half *Bottom Half*

10. Divide Trees into two separate stacks of ten according to Trunk color. Press seams in first stack away from top of Tree.

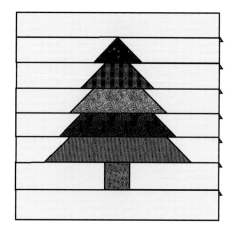

11. Press seams in second stack toward top of Tree.

12. Square up block.

Center at 6¼" line. Trim two sides.

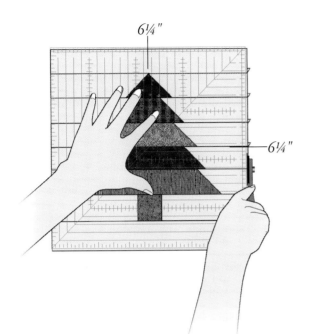

Center at 3¼" line. Trim two sides.

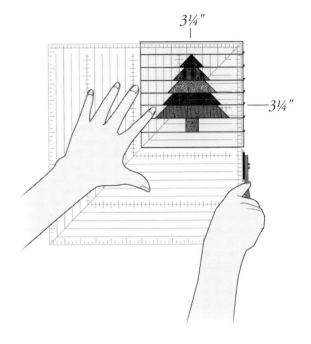

*Turn block. Center at 6¼" line.
Trim remaining two sides.*

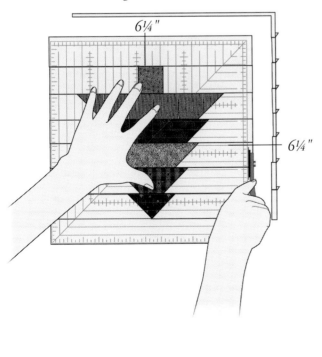

*Turn block. Center at 3¼" line.
Trim remaining two sides.*

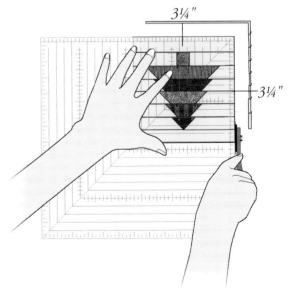

Twenty Block Tree Quilt

Yardage and Cutting for Twenty Trees

In addition to the yardage requirements for 20 Tree blocks on page 41, you need the following fabrics to finish this quilt. See pages 42-55 for sewing instructions.

Lattice ────────────
⅔ yd
(11) 2½" strips into
(31) 2½" x 12½"

Cornerstones ────────
⅛ yd
(1) 2½" strip
(12) 2½" squares

First Border ────────
½ yd
(7) 2" strips

Second Border ────────
1 yd
(8) 4½" strips

Binding ────────
¾ yd
(8) 3" strips

Batting ────────
4 yds

Backing ────────
68" x 84"

Approximate Finished Size 64" x 77½" (12" Finished Block)
Sue Bouchard

Twelve Block Tree Quilt

See pages 42-55 for sewing instructions.

Twelve Different Greens ────────
⅛ yd of each
(1) 2" strip from each

One Trunk ────────────
⅛ yd
(1) 2" strip

Background ────────────
2 yds
(2) 6" strips
(8) 2¼" strips
(18) 2" strips

Lattice ──────────────
⅞ yd
(6) 2" strips
(17) 2" x 12½"
(6) 2" strips

Cornerstones ────────────
⅛ yd
(1) 2" strip
(6) 2" squares

First Border ────────────
1 yd
(6) 4½" strips

Binding ────────────────
¾ yd
(7) 3" strips

Batting ────────────────
56" x 70"

Backing ────────────────
58" x 72"

Approximate Finished Size 51" x 63"
Sue Bouchard

The twelve block Tree quilt was made from pre-washed flannel fabrics. Construction of the Tree block is completed in the same order except the different Tree fabrics are not mixed up. Each Tree is completed from a single fabric.

Caribou Crossing

Six Different Greens ⎯⎯⎯⎯⎯⎯⎯⎯
⅛ yd of each
(1) 2" strip from each

One Trunk ⎯⎯⎯⎯⎯⎯⎯⎯
⅛ yd
(1) 2" x 10" piece

Background ⎯⎯⎯⎯⎯⎯⎯⎯
1 yd
(1) 6" strip
(4) 2¼" strips
(9) 2" strips

Lattice ⎯⎯⎯⎯⎯⎯⎯⎯
½ yd
(3) 2" strips
    (7) 2" x 12½"
(4) 2" strips

Cornerstones ⎯⎯⎯⎯⎯⎯⎯⎯
⅛ yd
(2) 2" squares

Border ⎯⎯⎯⎯⎯⎯⎯⎯
⅝ yd
(4) 4½" strips

Binding ⎯⎯⎯⎯⎯⎯⎯⎯
½ yd
(5) 3" strips

Batting ⎯⎯⎯⎯⎯⎯⎯⎯
44" x 57"

Backing ⎯⎯⎯⎯⎯⎯⎯⎯
46" x 60"

Optional Caribou Applique
¼ yd Caribou Fabric
¼ yd Paper Backed Fusible Interfacing

Approximate Finished Size 38" x 51"
Sue Bouchard

1. Make six Tree blocks.
   See pages 42-55.

2. Lay out the blocks with lattice and cornerstones.

3. Assembly-line sew vertical rows.

4. Assembly-line sew horizontal rows, pushing seams toward lattice.

Optional: Applique Caribou on the quilt top. The Caribou pattern is on page 60. See page 13 for using paper-backed fusible interfacing.

5. Add borders to long sides first, and then top and bottom.

6. Finish quilt. See pages 122-128.

Caribou and Star
Patterns

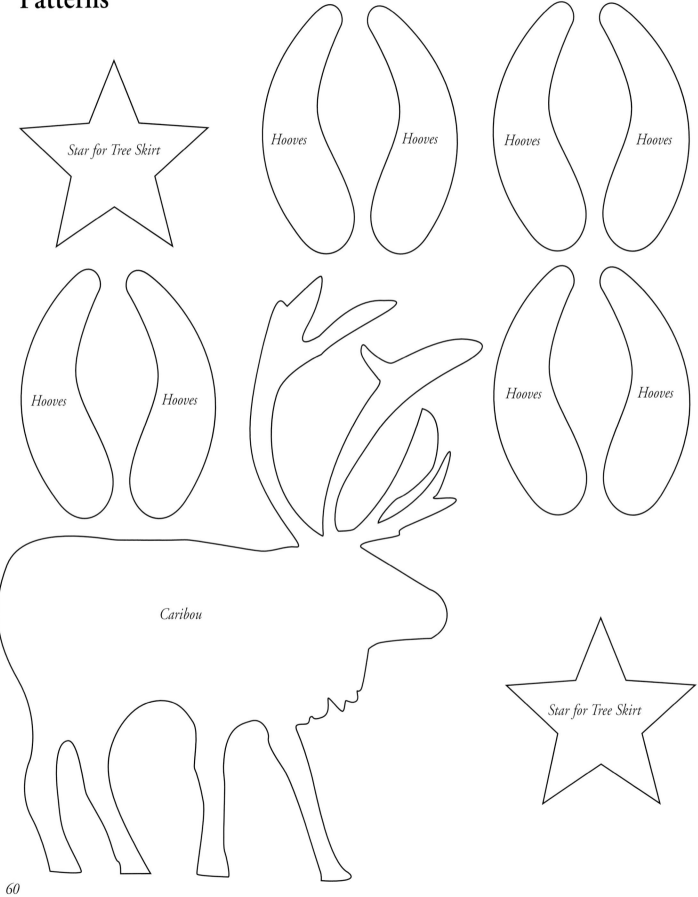

Star for Tree Skirt

Hooves   Hooves

Hooves   Hooves

Hooves   Hooves

Hooves   Hooves

Caribou

Star for Tree Skirt

60

Tree Ornaments

Use the trimmings from the Tree strips. See page 47.

Approximate Finished Size
3½" square
Eleanor Burns

Making Triangle Pieced Squares

1. Assembly-line sew the trimmings right sides together with a seam slightly less than ¼". *If you save and sew all of them, there are 200.*

2. Peel away the ornament's static triangle pattern from the protective paper. See back of book. *Triangle is half a 1¼" square.*

3. Place it on the underside corner of your 6" square ruler.

4. Line up the triangle's diagonal line with the stitching line. Line up an edge of the ruler with one straight side of the block. Trim.

5. Trim off seam allowance corners.

6. Open and press seams to the dark side.

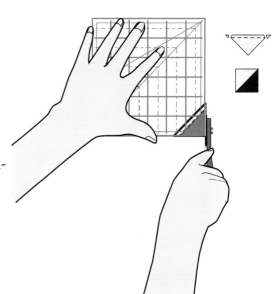

Making the Patterns

There are many different ways to lay out the miniature blocks. Here are a few to get you started.

1. Lay out blocks.

2. Sew together with a seam slightly less than ¼". These measurements are approximate, based on your seam allowance.

3. Square blocks to 3¾".

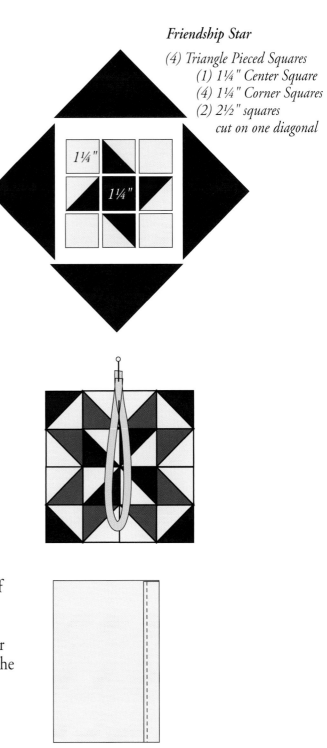

Friendship Star

(4) Triangle Pieced Squares
   (1) 1¼" Center Square
   (4) 1¼" Corner Squares
   (2) 2½" squares
     cut on one diagonal

Finishing the Ornament

1. To finish each ornament, cut these pieces:
   (2) 3" x 3¾" pieces backing
   (1) 3¼" square thin cotton batting
   (1) 6" piece ¼" ribbon or jute

2. Fold and pin the ribbon or jute on the patchwork.

3. Turn under and edgestitch the 3¾" sides of the backing.

4. Place the backing pieces right sides together to the patchwork. Overlap the backing in the center.

5. Sew around the outside edge with a seam slightly less than ¼".

6. Place the batting on patchwork side. Roll and turn right side out.

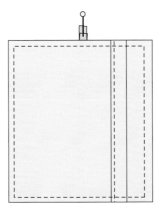

Morning Star

(1) 2¼" Center Square
(8) Triangle Pieced Squares
    Sew pairs together first
(4) 1¼" Corner Squares

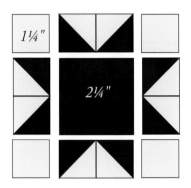

Barbara Frietchie Star

(16) Triangle Pieced Squares

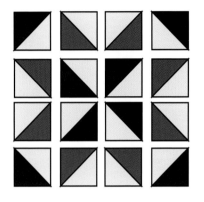

Maple Leaf

(4) Triangle Pieced Squares
(3) 1¼" Center Squares
(2) 1¼" Background Squares
    Edgestitch narrow
    Stem on one
(2) 2½" Squares
    Cut on one diagonal

Geese in Flight

(9) Triangle Pieced Squares
(2) 2½" Squares
    cut on one diagonal

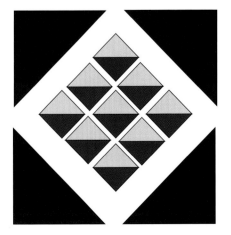

Tablecloth or Tree Skirt

Approximate Size 36" Across Center

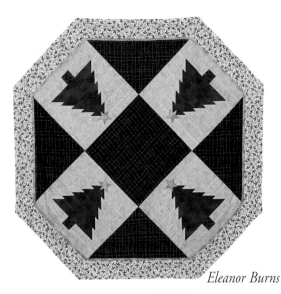

Eleanor Burns

Eleanor Burns

Teresa Varnes

Tree —————————————————————
　1/3 yd
　　　(4) 2" strips

Trunk —————————————————————
　1/8 yd
　　　(1) 2" x 10" piece

Tree Background ——————————————
　3/4 yd
　　　(3) 2¼" strips
　　　(6) 2" strips
　　　(1) 6" strip
　　　　(2) 6" x 10" pieces

Main Fabric ————————————————
　5/8 yd
　　　(1) 12½" square
　　　(1) 18" square
　　　　Cut into fourths on both diagonals

Folded Border ————————————————
　1/4 yd
　　　(4) 1¼" strips

Border ——————————————————————
　2/3 yd
　　　(4) 3½" strips

Backing —————————————————————
　1¼ yds

Lightweight Batting ——————————————
　1¼ yds

Optional Applique ——————————————
　1/4 yd fabric
　1/4 yd paper backed fusible interfacing

Cutting Four Tree Blocks

1. Open four green 2" strips. Layer selvage to selvage, right side up.

2. Using a rotary cutter, remove selvages from left end.

Cut four segments from largest to smallest.

3. Place segments in Tree layout as you cut.

4. Open and layer the three 2¼" Background strips right side up.

5. Cut into eight 13" lengths.

6. Layer two folded 2" Background strips at a time.

7. Cut two stacks of four segments each, and place in Tree layout.

Two Stacks of Four Segments Each

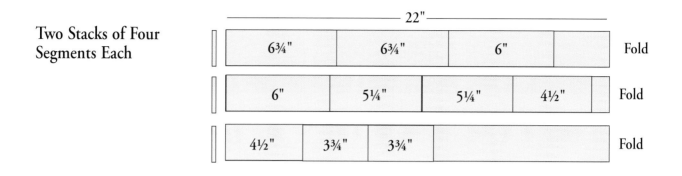

8. Turn all segments right sides up.

9. Mark and sew four Tree blocks following the directions on pages 45-55.

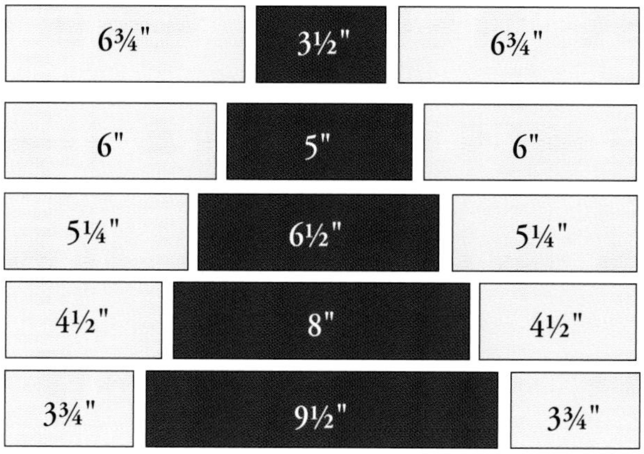

6¾"	3½"	6¾"
6"	5"	6"
5¼"	6½"	5¼"
4½"	8"	4½"
3¾"	9½"	3¾"

Appliqueing Options

It's best to decorate with stars, caribou, or any shape you desire, before sewing the tree skirt together. See page 13 for appliqueing instructions.

Stars: Trace and cut four, fuse to tree, and applique.

Caribou: Trace and cut. Center on Main Fabric triangles, leaving room for seam allowance. Fuse and applique.

Sewing the Top Together

1. Lay out the four Tree blocks with the 12½" Main Fabric square and triangles cut from the 18" Main Fabric square.

2. Flip the middle row to the first row.

3. Match the square edges. Let the tips of the triangles hang over.

4. Assembly-line sew. Do not clip the connecting threads.

5. Flip the third row to the middle row. Assembly-line sew. Do not clip the connecting threads.

6. Sew the center rows, finger pressing the seams away from the Tree blocks.

7. Press.

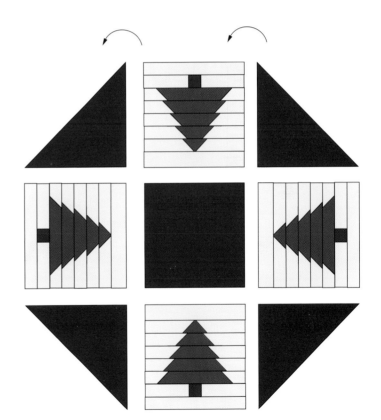

Adding the Folded Border

1. Press the 1¼" folded border strips **wrong sides** together.

2. Match folded border raw edges with raw edge of top. Sew with 6-8 stitches per inch, and a ⅛" seam allowance.

3. At each angle, cut and overlap new piece.

Adding the 3½" Border

1. Cut one 12½" piece from each of the four 3½" strips.

2. Sew 12½" pieces to bottoms of all Tree blocks. Press seams away from block.

3. Draw 45º lines on ends of 12½" strips. Lines should match up with the cut edges of the folded border.

4. Line up remaining strips on 45º lines, pin, and sew.

5. Trim excess on 45º angle.

6. Press seams toward border.

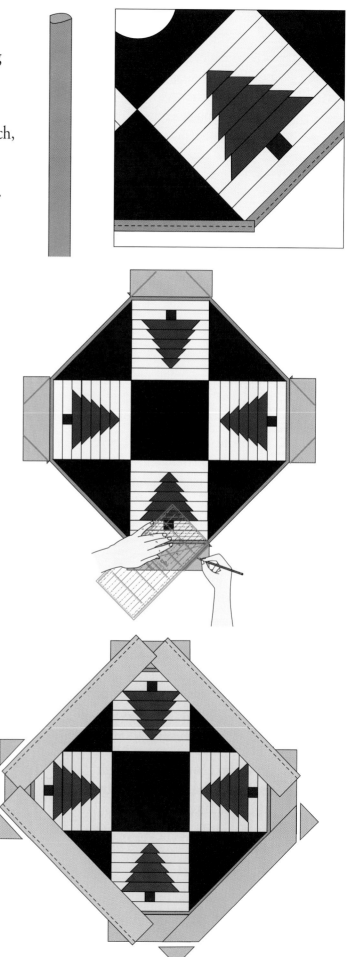

Marking the Hole in the Tree Skirt Only

1. Find a bowl or dish the same size as your tree trunk. A bowl with a 7" diameter is a good size.

2. Center bowl on **wrong side of Tree Skirt**. Trace.

3. Draw a line from center to outside edge.

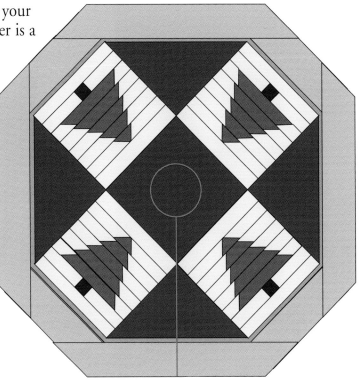

Quick Turning

1. Place top right sides together to backing.

2. Pin around the outside edge, and trim. Stitch, leaving an 8"opening.

   Tree Skirt Only - Stitch ¼" from center line, and on the circle line. Cut on the center line, and ¼" from the circle line.

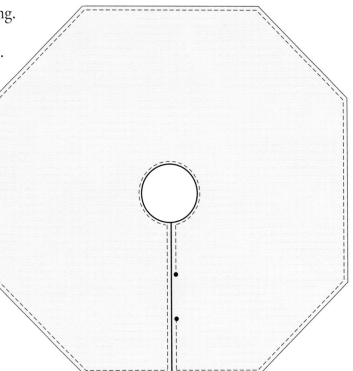

3. Place on top of batting. Trim batting to size.

4. Whipstitch batting to outside edge.

5. Turn right side out through opening.

6. Slipstitch opening shut.

Bear's Paw Wallhanging
Sue Bouchard

the Bear's Paw

Bear Valley
Sue Bouchard

Yardage and Cutting Chart for Four Bear's Paw Blocks

This is a repeat of the yardage on page 9.

	Full Size 12" Finished Block	Wallhanging 6" Finished Block

Background	⅔ yd
	(1) 2¼" strip
	    (16) 2¼" squares
	(2) 6" strips
	    (4) 6" x 12" rectangles
	(3) 2" strips
	    (16) 2" x 5¾" rectangles
		¼ yd
		(1) 1⅜" strip
		    (16) 1⅜" squares
		(2) 4" strips
		    (4) 4" x 8" rectangles
		(3) 1¼" strips
		    (16) 1¼" x 3⅛" rectangles

Bear's Claws	⅜ yd
	(2) 6" strips
	    (4) 6" x 12" rectangles
		¼ yd
		(1) 4" strip
		    (4) 4" x 8" rectangles

Bear's Paw	⅓ yd
	(2) 4" strips
	    (16) 4" squares
		⅛ yd
		(1) 2¼" strip
		    (16) 2¼" squares

Center Square	⅛ yd
	(1) 2" x 10"
	    (4) 2" squares
		⅛ yd
		(1) 1¼" x 6"
		    (4) 1¼" squares

Making the Triangle Pieced Squares for the Bear's Claws

 1. Place a Background rectangle right sides together to a Claw rectangle. Place the lightest fabric on top, wrong side up. Press.

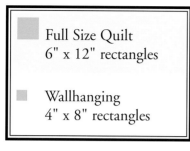

Full Size Quilt
6" x 12" rectangles

Wallhanging
4" x 8" rectangles

2. Place on a gridded cutting mat.

3. Using the grid, draw vertical lines. Draw one horizontal line across center.

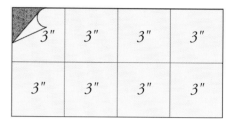

Example of a Full Size Quilt

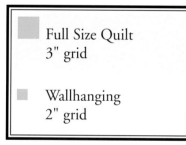

Full Size Quilt
3" grid

Wallhanging
2" grid

4. Beginning in the bottom right corner, draw diagonal lines every other square.

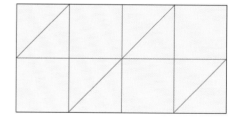

5. Draw diagonal lines in the opposite direction in the unmarked squares.

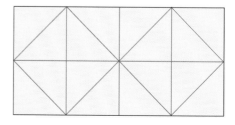

6. Continuously sew ¼" from the diagonal line. Pivot and turn the rectangle as you sew, until you get back to where you started.

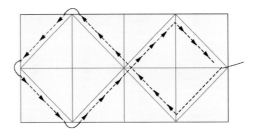

7. Continuously sew ¼" from the diagonal line on the second side.

8. Set seams by pressing the two fabrics together.

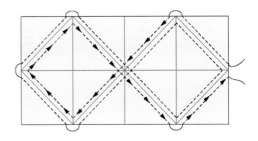

9. Cut apart on the vertical and horizontal lines. Cut on the diagonal lines.

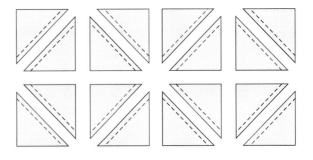

Squaring the Claws

Two different methods are described. Read and test both methods before selecting one.

Static Paper Method

Static Paper is provided in the back of this book.

1. Find the static pattern paper in the back of the book. Select the triangle pattern for your size quilt. Peel from the protective paper.

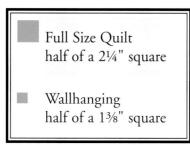

   ■ Full Size Quilt
   half of a 2¼" square

   ■ Wallhanging
   half of a 1⅜" square

2. Place the static paper triangle on the underside corner of your 6" square ruler. Match the outside edges.

3. Line up the triangle's diagonal line with the stitching line. Line up an edge of the ruler with one straight side of the block. Trim.

   If you are unable to line up ruler with a straight side, center the template on the triangle. Trim on two sides.

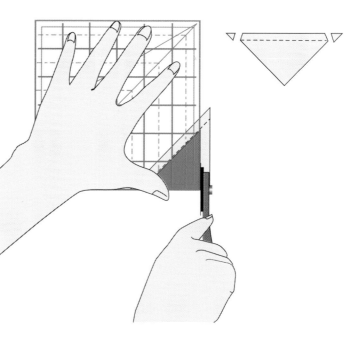

4. Trim off seam allowance corners.

5. Place on pressing mat with Claw fabric on top. Open and **finger press seam toward Claw fabric. Gently touch the iron to the seam.**

6. Adjust the static paper if patch is not square.

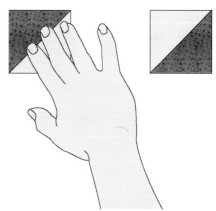

   ■ Full Size Quilt
   2¼" square

   ■ Wallhanging
   1⅜" square

Squaring Up with 6" Ruler

1. Press seam allowances toward Background.

2. Place the 6" Square Up ruler on the Claw so the desired measurement is centered on the patch. Trim on two sides.

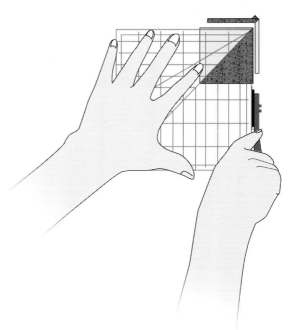

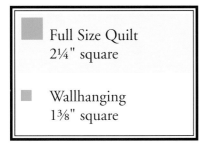

Full Size Quilt
2¼" square

Wallhanging
1⅜" square

3. Turn Claw and place measurement of desired size square on cut edges. Cut remaining two sides, squaring the patch.

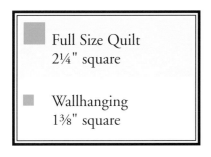

Full Size Quilt
2¼" square

Wallhanging
1⅜" square

Making Four Stacks

1. Make four stacks of 16 Triangle Pieced Squares in each. Turn two stacks in one direction.

2. Turn two stacks in a second direction.

Making the Paws

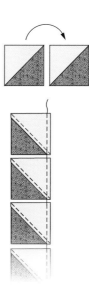

1. Select first two stacks. Flip piece on right to piece on left. Assembly-line sew patches together.

   Use stiletto to help feed pieces and match edges.

2. Clip apart every four. Drop on pressing mat with stitches **across bottom**. Set seams. Open and press flat. Clip apart.

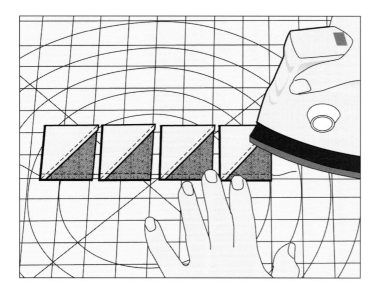

Seam is pressed to left.

3. Lay out Claws with stacks of Paws and Background squares.

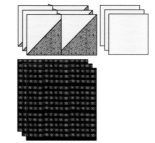

Full Size Quilt - 4" Paws and 2¼" Background square

Wallhanging - 2¼" Paws and 1⅜" Background square

4. Check the placement of diagonal seams on remaining two stacks of Claws.

5. Assembly-line sew patches together.

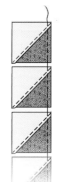

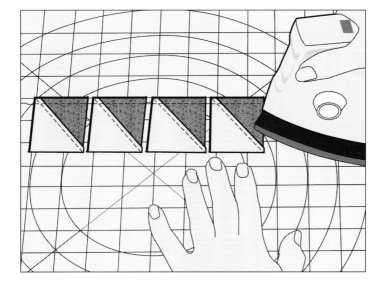

Seam is pressed to right.

6. Clip apart in groups of four.

7. Drop on pressing mat with stitches **across top**. Set seams. Open and press flat. Clip apart.

8. Add second set of Claws to layout. You should have 16 pieces in each stack for four Bear's Paw blocks.

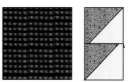

Sewing Paw and Claws Together

1. Flip Background square right sides together to two Claws and sew.

2. Flip two Claws right sides together to Paw and assembly-line sew, alternating between two, until all pieces have been sewn together.

3. Clip threads every two pieces.

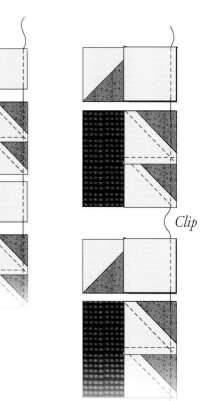

Clip

4. Flip right sides together. Finger press the seams on top toward the Background, and the seams underneath toward the Paw. Lock the seams.

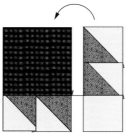
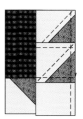

5. Assembly-line sew all Paws.

6. Press final seam toward Paw.

7. Square up. Be careful to leave seam allowance.

Full Size Quilt
5¾" square

Wallhanging
3⅛" square

Completing the Bear's Paw Block

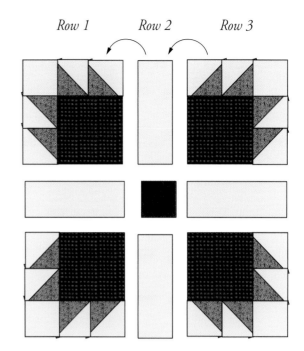

1. Lay out all the pieces required to complete the Bear's Paw Block.

2. Flip the middle row onto the first row. Assembly-line sew. Flip the third row onto the middle row. Assembly-line sew. Press seam allowances towards Background.

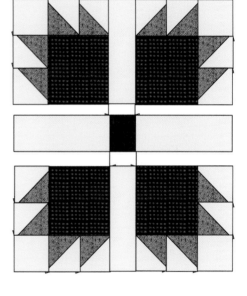

3. Sew center rows together. Press seams toward Background and Center.

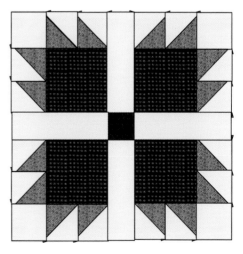

Bear's Paw Wallhanging

Yardage and Cutting Chart for Four Block Bear's Paw

In addition to the yardage for the four Bear's Paws blocks on page 71, you need the following fabrics to finish this quilt.

Lattice _____
⅓ yd
    (4) 2" strips
      (12) 2" x 12½"

Cornerstones _____
⅛ yd
    (1) 2" strip
      (9) 2" x 2"

First Border _____
⅓ yd
    (4) 2¼" strips

Second Border _____
½ yd
    (4) 4" strips

Binding _____
⅜ yd
    (4) 3" strips

Batting _____
43" x 43"

Backing _____
45" x 45"

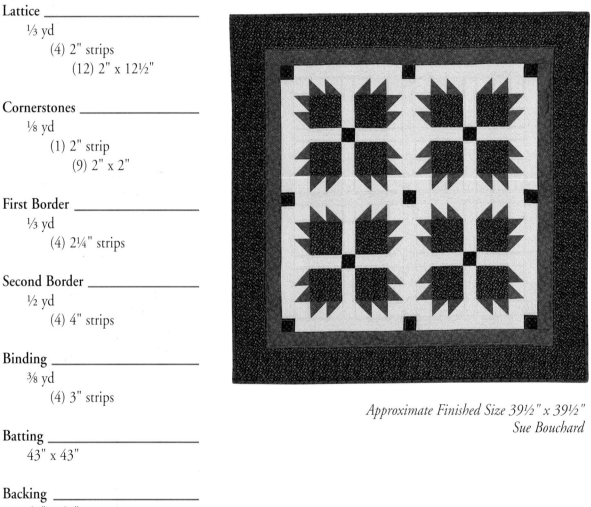

Approximate Finished Size 39½" x 39½"
Sue Bouchard

1. Make four Bears Paw blocks. See pages 71-79.

2. Lay out the blocks with lattice and cornerstones.

3. Assembly-line sew vertical rows.

4. Assembly-line sew horizontal rows, pushing seams toward lattice.

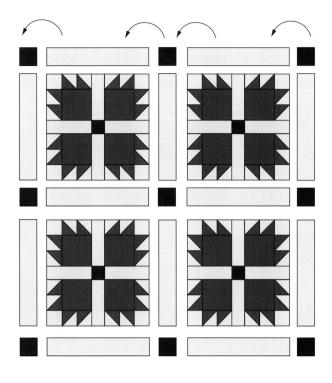

5. Add borders and binding.

   Optional: Applique Bears on the borders.

Bear Valley Wallhanging

Approximate Finished Size 36" x 36"
16 Paws from 12" Finished Block
Sue Bouchard

This antique twenty block Bear's Paw quilt was made in the late 1800's out of solid turkey red fabric. Because turkey red required a multi-stage dyeing process, it was often priced considerably higher than other fabrics sold for clothing and quilts. In the 1875-76 Montgomery Ward catalog, quilt-makers could order red prints for 9½ cents a yard, or Turkey Red prints for 27½ cents a yard. Perhaps the rust colored lattice was originally a synthetic red dye that turned to brown.

Journalist and political activist, Ruth Finley, identified the block in Old Patchwork Quilts, and the Women Who Made Them. Since the 1800's in western Pennsylvania and Ohio, the block was identified as Bear's Paw. However, on Long Island, the pattern was referred to as "Duck's Foot in the Mud." The Society of Friends in Philadelphia referred to the same pattern as Hand of Friendship.

Yardage and Cutting

Center Picture

Ground	¼ yd	(1) 6½" x 18½"
Sky	¾ yd	(1) 12½" x 18½"
Mountains	¼ yd	(1) 7" x 18½"
Trees	(3) ¼ yd pieces	(1) 6" x 8" from each
Trunks	⅛ yd	(1) 3" x 8"
Bears	¼ yd	(1) 6" x 8"
Paper Backed Fusible Interfacing	1 yd	

Borders

First Border	¼ yd	(3) 2½" strips
Folded Border	¼ yd	(4) 1¼" strips

Bear Paws Border

Background	½ yd	(1) 2¼" strip into
		  (16) 2¼" squares
		(2) 6" strips into
		  (4) 6" x 12" rectangles

Claws	⅜ yd	(2) 6" strips into (4) 6" x 12" rectangles
Paw	¼ yd	(2) 4" strips into (16) 4" squares

Inside Triangles	⅓ yd	(3) 8½" x 8½"
		  cut on both diagonals
		(2) 4½" squares
		  cut on one diagonal

Outside Triangles	½ yd	Cut (1) 8½" strip into
		  (3) 8½" squares
		    cut on both diagonals
		(1) 4½" strip
		  (6) 4½" squares
		    cut on one diagonal

Finishing

Backing	42" square	
Batting	41" square	
Binding	½ yd	(5) 3" strips

Making the Side Bear's Paw Borders

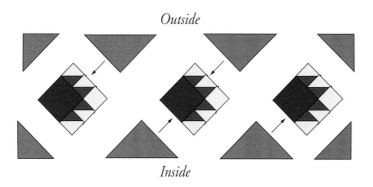

1. Make 16 Bear's Paws following directions on pages 71-79.

2. Lay out all the pieces required to complete the side borders.
   Place two pieces in each stack.

3. Match square edges. Assembly-line sew large triangles to the sides of the Bear's Paws.

Outside

Inside

4. Center and sew two small triangles to the Bear's Paw patches. Fold out.

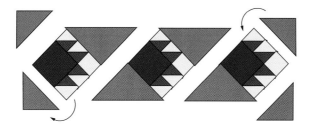

5. Center and sew two remaining triangles.

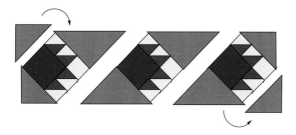

6. Sew the Bear's Paws units together to complete the side borders.

Completing the Top and Bottom Bear's Paw Borders

1. Lay out all the pieces required to complete the top and bottom borders. Place two pieces in each stack.

2. Assembly-line sew the large triangles to the sides of the Bear's Paws.

3. Sew the small triangles to the Bear's Paws.

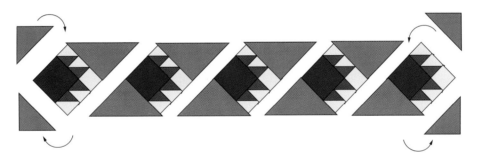

4. Sew the Bear's Paws units together to complete the top and bottom borders.

Making the Applique

1. Trace the Bears, Trees, and Mountains on the paper side of the fusible interfacing. See pages 90-91.

2. Cut pieces apart according to color.

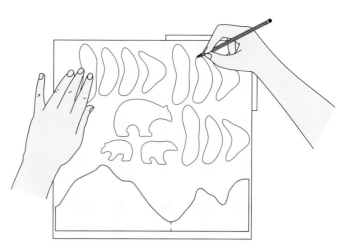

3. Bond the interfacing to the **wrong side** of each fabric.

4. Cut out the shapes on the lines.

5. Peel the paper away.

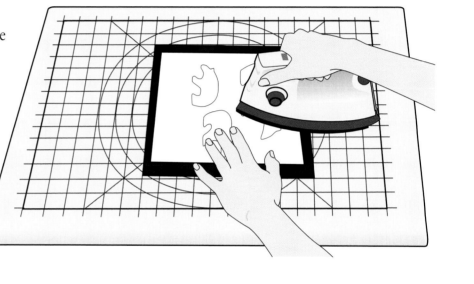

Completing the Center Picture

1. Line up the bottom raw edges of the Mountain and the Sky. Bond the Mountains to the Sky. Machine applique the top edge of the Mountain.

   See page 13 for Applique methods.

2. With right sides together, sew the Sky piece to the Ground.

3. Press seam allowances toward the Ground.

4. Fuse paper backed interfacing to wrong side of Trunk fabric.

5. Cut Trunk fabric into (3) ½" x 8" strips. Taper the Tree tops to ¼" width.

6. Fuse Trunks to Sky/Ground piece. Applique in place.

7. Fuse the Tree pieces and the Bears as shown. Applique in place.

Adding the First Border

1. Sew the 2½" First Border to the center picture. Add the sides first, then the top and bottom.

2. Press seam allowances toward the First Border.

Adding the Folded Border

A Folded Border is a folded, narrow strip of fabric to be sewn between any two borders for accent color.

1. Press the 1¼" strips in half lengthwise, **wrong sides** together.

2. Measure the sides of the quilt, and cut two strips this measurement.

3. Match and pin raw edges of quilt and Folded Border. Sew with a seam two threads less than ¼". Use a long stitch or 6-8 stitches per inch.

4. Measure top and bottom, and cut two strips this measurement.

5. Pin and sew to the quilt. Do not fold out.

Adding the Bear's Paw Border

1. Add the two side Bear's Paw strips to the left and right side of the quilt. Make sure you have the Paws going in the correct direction. Press seam allowances away from the center.

2. Add the top and bottom Bear's Paw strips to the quilt. Make sure you have the Paws going in the correct direction. Press seam allowances away from the center.

3. Quilt and bind.

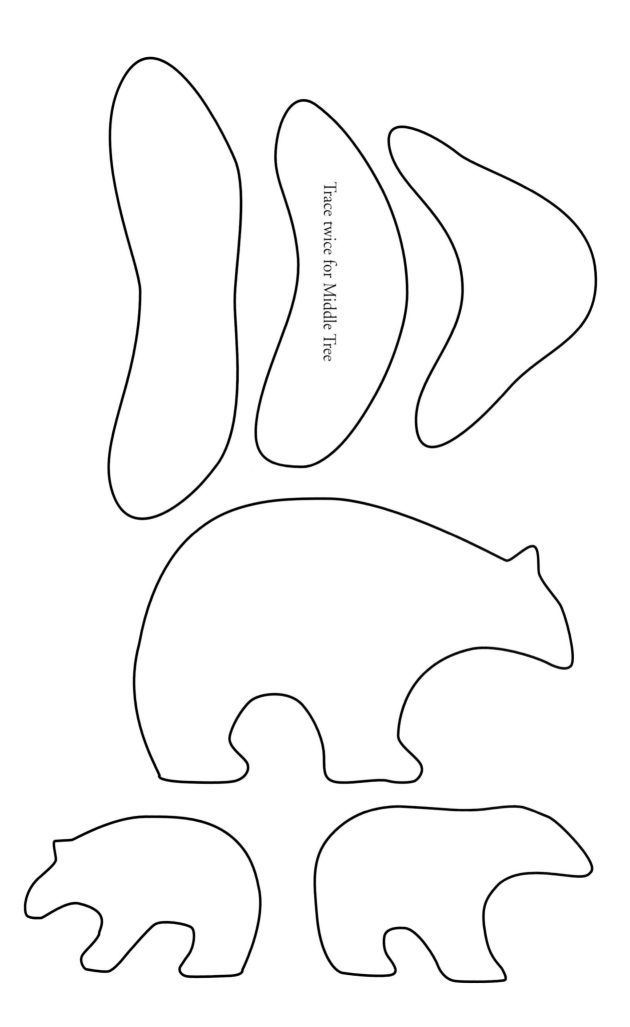

Trace twice for Middle Tree

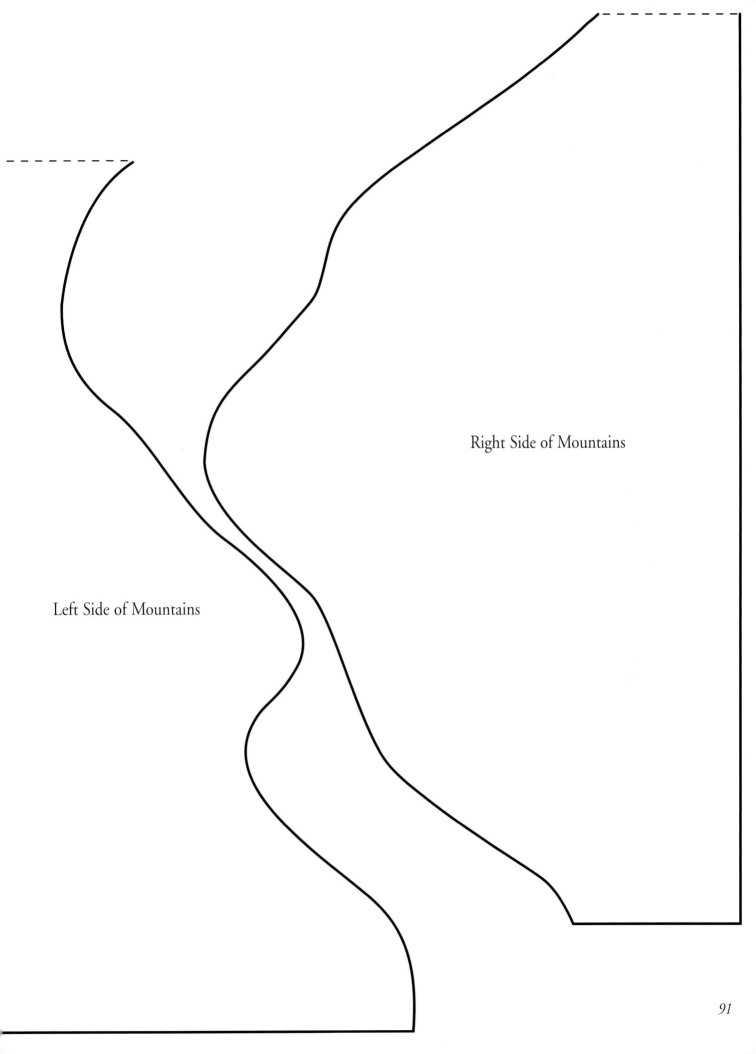

Right Side of Mountains

Left Side of Mountains

Quilt Box
Sue Bouchard

the Flying Geese

Migrating Geese
Sue Bouchard

Cabin in the Pines
Sue Bouchard

Yardage and Cutting Chart for 104 Geese Blocks

This is a repeat of the yardage on page 9.

	Full Size 3" x 6" Finished Block	Wallhanging 1½" x 3" Finished Block
Background	2¼ yds (8) 9" strips (32) 9" squares	1¼ yds (6) 6" strips (32) 6" squares
Eight Different Darks	¼ yd of each From each fabric (1) 7½" strip (4) 7½" squares	¼ yd of each From each fabric (1) 4½" strip (4) 4½" squares

Flying Geese patches became popular the second quarter of the 19th century. The quiltmaker cut 4½" and 3½" squares on one diagonal, and then stitched the smaller triangles to the larger one, making the outside edge on the larger piece on the bias!

The Geese in this straight setting features the "oil red, oil green, and violent yellow" that Marie Webster referred to with disdain.

Wild Goose Chase features patches in indigo blues and reds with shirting, and is set together with squares cut from an old apron.

Examine Your Rulers

This method works best with a 6" x 12" ruler with

- 45º line

- ¼" line

Use this ruler for lining the diagonal line on the seam, and accurately cutting a ¼" seam. Page 97.

6" x 12" Ruler

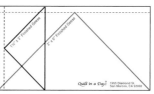

Geese Square Up Ruler

As an alternate to the static paper method of squaring geese, use this heavy ruler with necessary markings.

Use a 12½" Square Up Ruler with a 45º line and a ¼" line for cutting squares and squaring Full Size Geese. Page 98

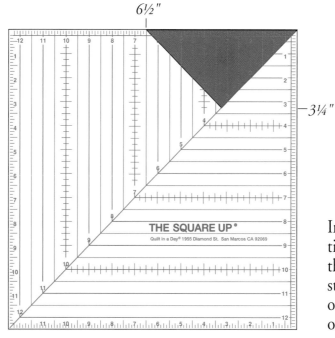

12½" Square Up Ruler

6" Square Ruler for squaring Wallhanging Size Geese

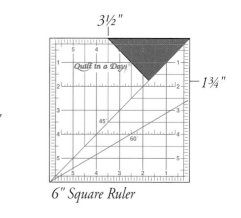

6" Square Ruler

In the back of this book is blue static paper. Peel away the pattern for the size Geese you are making, and stick the pattern on the under side of your ruler. Carefully match the outside edges and diagonal lines.

Flying Geese

 1. Place the smaller square right sides together and centered on the larger square. Press.

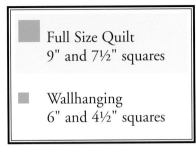

Full Size Quilt
9" and 7½" squares

Wallhanging
6" and 4½" squares

Each set makes four Geese.

2. With the 6" x 24" ruler, draw a diagonal line across the squares. Pin.

3. Sew exactly ¼" from both sides of drawn line. Press to set seam.

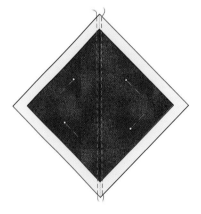

4. Cut on drawn line. **Press seam allowance to larger triangle.**

5. Place squares right sides together so that opposite fabrics touch.

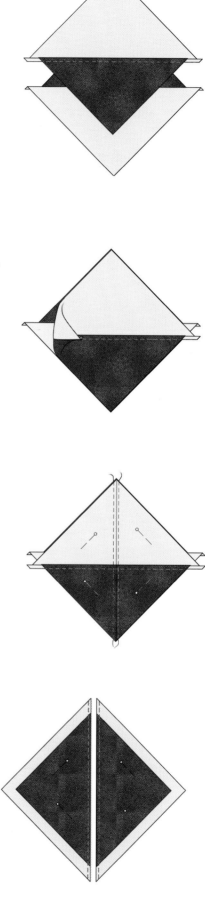

6. **Match up the outside edges.** Notice that there is a gap between the seams. The seams **do not lock.**

7. Draw a diagonal line across the seams. Pin.

8. Sew ¼" from both sides of drawn line. Press to set seam.

9. Cut on the drawn line.

10. Clip the seam allowance to the vertical seam midway between the horizontal seams. This allows the seam allowance to be pressed to the fabric of the original larger square.

11. Press each half open, pushing the clipped seam allowance to the fabric of the larger square.

12. With a 6" x 12" ruler, line up the 45º line on a Geese seam, and the ¼" line on the peak.

13. Cut across, keeping an exact ¼" seam allowance beyond each peak.

14. Turn second piece and repeat. A small strip will be cut out of center. Stack. Set the 6" x 12" ruler aside.

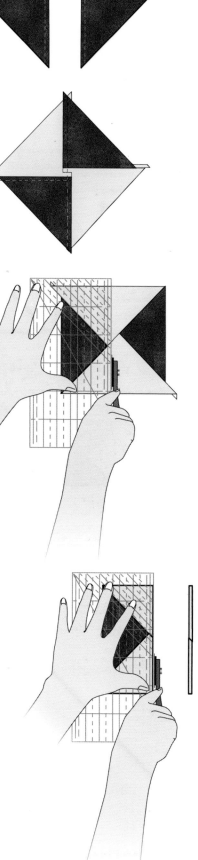

Full Size Quilt 3½" x 6½"

Wallhanging 2" x 3½"

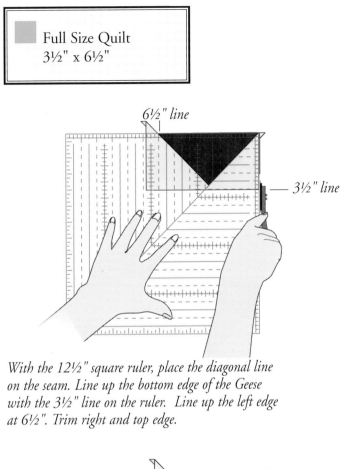

With the 12½" square ruler, place the diagonal line on the seam. Line up the bottom edge of the Geese with the 3½" line on the ruler. Line up the left edge at 6½". Trim right and top edge.

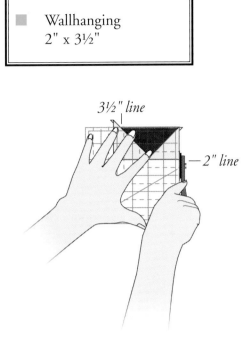

With the 6" square ruler, place the diagonal line on the seam. Line up the bottom edge of the Geese with the 2" line on the ruler. Line up the left edge at 3½". Trim right and top edge.

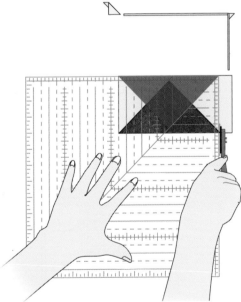

Turn and trim right edge to a perfect 3½" x 6½".

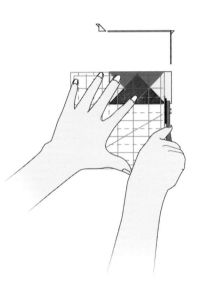

Turn and trim right edge to a perfect 2" x 3½".

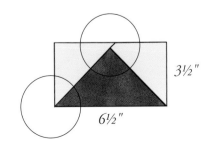

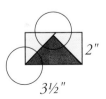

Migrating Geese

Yardage and Cutting Chart for 104 Geese Blocks

In addition to the yardage requirements on page 93, you need the following yardage to finish this quilt.
See pages 93-98 for sewing instructions.

Lattice _____
⅔ yd
    (3) 3½" strips
    (4) 2½" strips

First Border (sides only) _____
¾ yd
    (4) 4½" strips

Second Border _____
1⅜ yds
    (7) 6½" strips

Binding _____
¾ yd
    (7) 3" strips

Batting _____
60" x 96"

Backing _____
3½ yds

Geese from Full Size Quilt
Approximate Finished Size 54" x 89"
Sue Bouchard

Making the Flying Geese

1. Make 104 Flying Geese Patches following the instructions for the Full Size Quilt.

2. **Set aside eight Geese Patches.**

3. Stack the remaining 96 patches into two stacks of 48 Flying Geese patches. Mix up the Geese Patches so you will not be sewing like patches together.

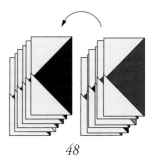

48

4. Assembly-line sew until you have 48 pairs sew together. Press seam allowance toward the base of the Geese Patch.

5. **Set aside four pairs for the four corners of the quilt.**

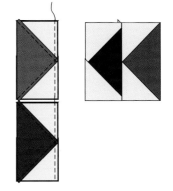

Sewing the Strips Together

1. In stacks of four, lay out pairs plus one extra Geese Patch. Make sure all patches are going in the same direction and like Geese fabrics are not next to each other.

2. Assembly-line sew the stacks together. Press seam allowances toward the base of the Geese.

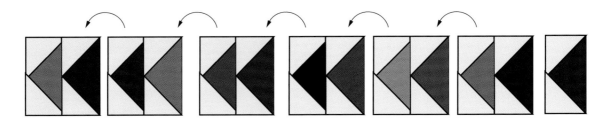

Four Center Strips - Six pairs plus one extra Geese - Thirteen Geese patches total.

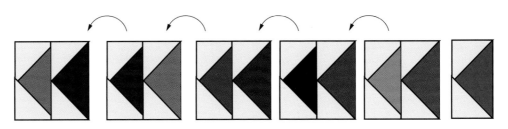

Two Top and Two Bottom Strips - Five Pairs plus one extra Geese - Eleven Geese patches total.

Sewing the Quilt Top Together

1. Lay out all the center strips so the Geese are going in the same direction.

2. Sew a 3½" lattice strip between rows of Geese. Press seams toward the lattice strips.

3. Measure the width of the sewn Center section and compare to the measurement of the eleven Geese strip.

4. If the two measurements are the same, go on to the next step. If the Center section is wider, take a wider seam allowance on the center lattice. If the Center section is smaller, make sure you used the correct width strips for the center lattice. If that was correct, take a smaller seam allowance on the center lattice.

Measure

Sewing the Sections Together

1. Cut four 2½" lattice strips to equal the length of the eleven geese strips.

2. Lay out geese strips with the lattice as shown. Sew and press the seams toward the lattice. Make two sets.

3. Sew lattice to the top and bottom of the Center section. Press seams toward lattice.

4. Sew top and bottom sections to the Center section. Press seams toward the lattice.

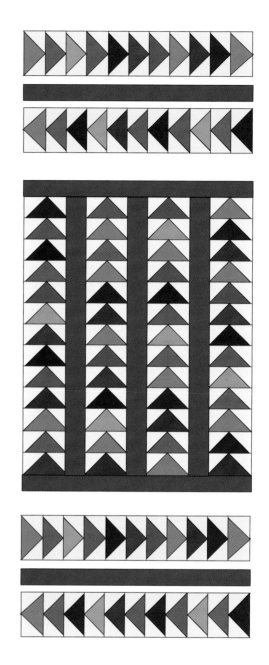

Adding the Borders

1. Sew two First Border strips together for each side. Measure the sides, and cut two.

2. Pin and sew to quilt top.

3. Sew two Second Border strips together for each side and 1½ strips for the top and bottom.

4. Measure the sides, top and bottom of your quilt and cut your border strips accordingly.

5. Pin and sew the side border strips to the quilt. Press seam allowances toward the border.

6. Sew one pair of Geese Patches to each end of the top and bottom border strips. Press seams toward the border.

7. Sew top and bottom border to the quilt. Press seam allowances toward the border.

8. Quilt and bind.

Cabin in the Pines Wallhanging

Approximate Finished Size 32" x 46"
Sue Bouchard

Approximate Finished Size 32" x 46"
Eleanor Burns

Yardage and Cutting

As you cut, sort pieces into piles for House (H), Star (S), and Trees (T). Background pieces are coded to help you sort. All measurements are given height by width.

House   ⅛ yd
- (1) 1½" x 6½"
- (1) 2½" x 3"
- (1) 2½" x 2"
- (1) 3½" x 6½"

Roof   ⅛ yd
- (1) 3½" x 6½"

Window   ⅛ yd
- (1) 2½" square

Star Points   ⅓ yd
- (1) 9" square

Star Center   ¼ yd
- (1) 6½" square

Trees   (6) ¼ yd pieces
- (1) 7½" square from each

Trunks   ⅛ yd
- (1) 1½" x 12" strip
- (4) 1½" x 12½" strips

Chimney and Smokestack
- (1) 3" square of each

Fusible Interfacing
- (1) 6" square

Log Pile
- (5) 2½" circles
- (1) 3" circle

Background   1⅛ yds
- (1) 13" strip
  - (1) 13" x 5" (H)
  - (2) 12½" x 3" (T)
  - (5) 12½" x 1½" (T)
  - (2) 12" x 3" (T)
  - (1) 9½" x 2½" (H)

- (2) 9" strips
  - (6) 9" squares (T)
  - (1) 7½" square (S)
  - (1) 4" x 8½" (H)

- (1) 3½" strip
  - (2) 3½" squares (H)
  - (4) 3½" squares (S)
  - (2) 3½" x 6½" (T)

Border   ½ yd
- (4) 4" strips

Batting   36" x 48"

Backing   1½ yd

Binding   ½ yd
- (4) 3" strips

Making the House

1. Draw a diagonal line on the wrong side of two 3½" Background squares.

2. Place marked Background square on the 3½" x 6½" Roof rectangle.

3. Sew on the drawn line.

4. Trim seam to ¼". Press seam toward Background.

5. Repeat process with the remaining 3½" Background square.

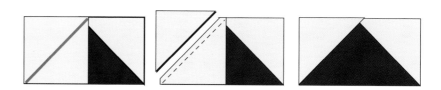

6. Sew 2½" x 3" House fabric to the left of Window square and 2½" x 2" House fabric to the right of the Window. Press seam allowances away from Window.

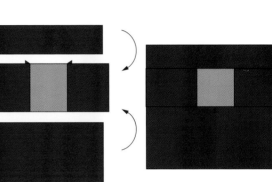

7. Sew 1½" x 6½" House to the top of Window and 3½" x 6½" House to the bottom of the Window. Press seams away from window unit.

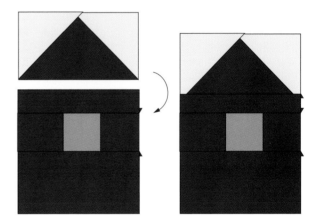

8. Flip roof right sides together to the house. Sew, and press seam toward the house.

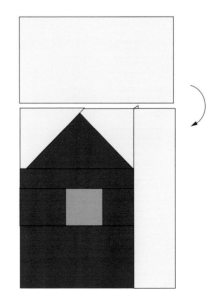

9. Flip 9½" x 2½" Background piece right sides together to the House. Sew and press seam toward Background fabric.

10. Flip 4" x 8½" Background fabric right sides together to the top of the House. Sew and press seam toward Background.

Applique Smoke Stack

Refer to the applique instructions on page 13.

Detail of Smoke Stack

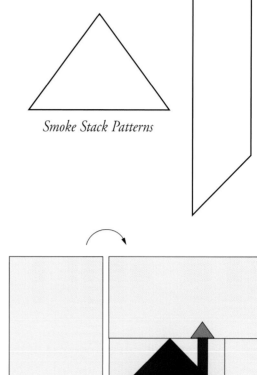

Smoke Stack Patterns

11. Flip 13" x 5" Background fabric right sides together to left side of House. Sew and press seam toward Background.

12. Using a Square-Up ruler, square block to 12½" x 12½".

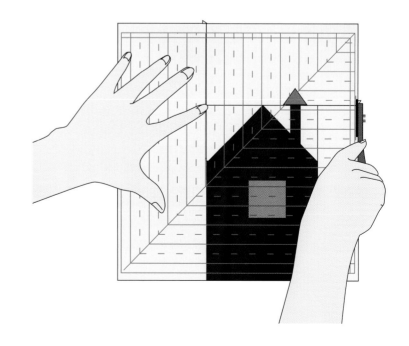

Making the Star

1. Center the 7½" Background square on the 9" Star Point square, right sides together.

2. Make the points of the Star following the Flying Geese instructions on pages 94-98.

3. Lay out the 6½" Center square, 3½" Corner squares and Points.

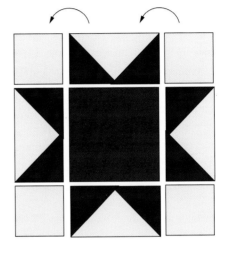

4. Flip the middle row to the left. Assembly-line sew the vertical seam.

5. Open and add the right row.

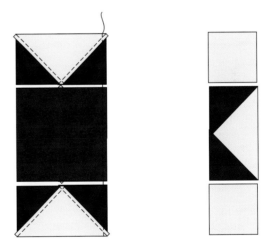

6. Sew the horizontal rows, pressing seams toward the Star Center, and away from the Star Points.

7. Press. Measure your block. It should measure 12½" square.

Making the Trees

1. Use the 7½" Tree squares and the 9" Background squares. Make the Trees following the Flying Geese instructions on pages 94-98.

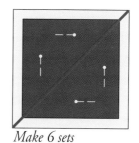

Make 6 sets

2. Sew a 12" x 3" Background strip to both sides of the 12" x 1½" Trunk strip. Press seam allowances toward the Trunk.

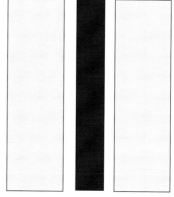

3. Measure. Pieces must measure 6½" wide. Adjust seam if necessary.

4. Cut (3) 3½" segments.

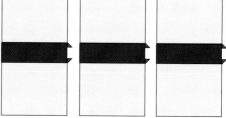

5. Mix up your green Geese Patches. Make three stacks of seven Geese in each stack. Point your Geese Patches toward the left. (You will have two Geese Patches left over.)

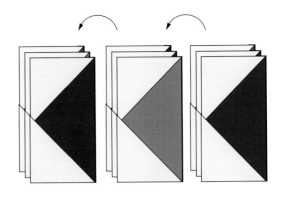

6. Assembly-line sew.

7. Press seam allowances toward the base of the Geese blocks.

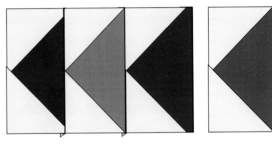

8. Add one more Geese Patch to the bottom of two units.

9. Add a 3½" x 6½" Background piece to the top of two units.

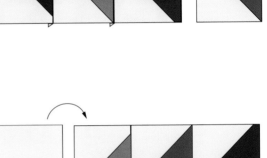

10. Add a Trunk unit to the bottom of the remaining three units.

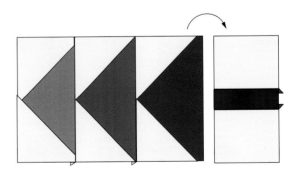

Finishing the Wallhanging

1. Lay out the 12½" x 1½" Background strips with Trees and Star for the top section of the quilt.

2. Sew and press seam allowances away from Trees and Stars.

3. Lay out the 12½" x 3" and 12½" x 1½" Background pieces with the 1½" x 12½" Trunk pieces for the bottom section of the quilt.

4. Sew and press the seam allowances away from Trees.

5. With right sides together, sew the top section to the bottom section. Press seam allowances toward the bottom section.

6. Add borders, quilt and bind.

Making a Log Pile

1. Double thread a hand sewing needle with quilting thread or regular matching thread. Knot the end.

2. Turn the edge of the fabric circle under ¼" to the wrong side, and baste.

3. Pull tight, push the needle through the middle to the back, and knot.

4. Before clipping the threads, sew to the side of the house in rows of three, two, and one.

Quilt Box

Yardage and Supply List

The instructions for the Quilt Box is based on using two Flying Geese Patches on each of the four sides of the box. But you can use the wallhanging Log Cabin Block, wallhanging Tree Block or the wallhanging Bear's Paw Block because they also are a 6" finished block.

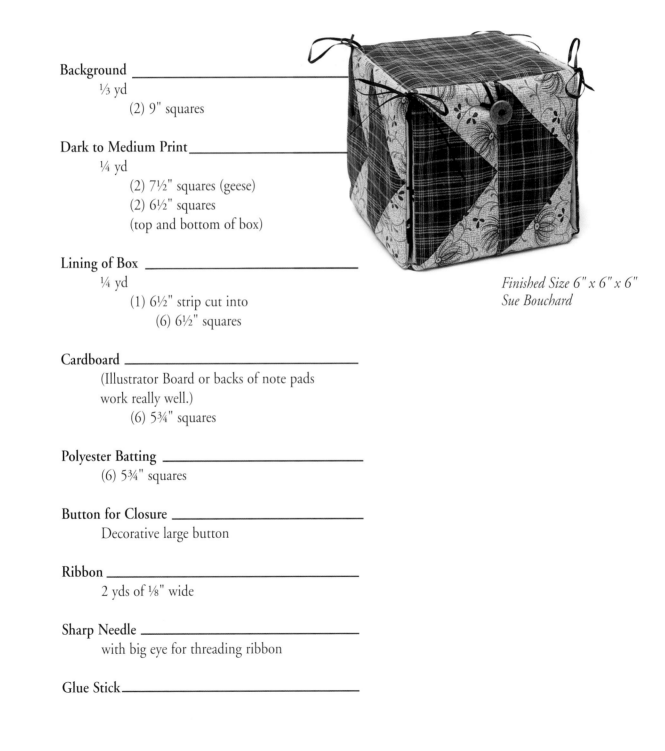

Background _____
    ⅓ yd
        (2) 9" squares

Dark to Medium Print _____
    ¼ yd
        (2) 7½" squares (geese)
        (2) 6½" squares
        (top and bottom of box)

Lining of Box _____
    ¼ yd
        (1) 6½" strip cut into
            (6) 6½" squares

Finished Size 6" x 6" x 6"
Sue Bouchard

Cardboard _____
    (Illustrator Board or backs of note pads
    work really well.)
        (6) 5¾" squares

Polyester Batting _____
    (6) 5¾" squares

Button for Closure _____
    Decorative large button

Ribbon _____
    2 yds of ⅛" wide

Sharp Needle _____
    with big eye for threading ribbon

Glue Stick _____

Preparing the Cardboard

1. Apply the glue stick along the outside edges of each piece of cardboard.

2. Place one square of batting on the cardboard. Set aside and allow to dry while sewing the box together.

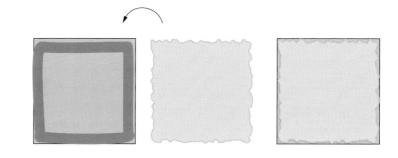

Sewing the Outside of the Box Together

1. Make eight Flying Geese patches using the technique shown on pages 93-98.

2. Make two stacks of four Flying Geese patches. Sew patches right sides together to make four pairs.

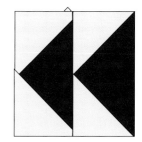

Stack four   *Stack four*

3. Lay out the Flying Geese pairs with top and bottom of your box.

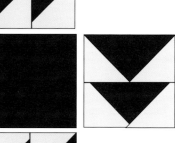

4. With right sides together, sew the left and right sides to the bottom of the quilt box. Press seam allowances away from the bottom.

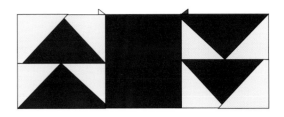

5. Line up edges of Geese on two opposite sides with bottom square seam allowances. Sew. Press seam allowances away from the bottom of the box.

6. Sew the top of the box to the left side. Press seam allowances toward the top of the box.

Sewing the Lining Together

1. Lay out the six lining squares in the same format as the outside of the box.

2. Sew squares together in the same order.

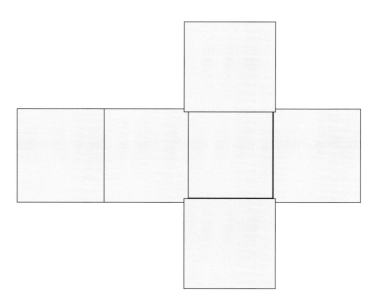

Sewing the Outside of the Box to the Lining

1. Layer the two pieces right sides together, making sure all the outside edges match. Pin at all the corners.

2. Sew the two pieces together, starting and stopping as shown.

3. Trim off corners. Clip down to seams at the corners of the bottom of the box.

4. Turn the fabrics right side out. Use a point turner to push out the corners. Press with an iron.

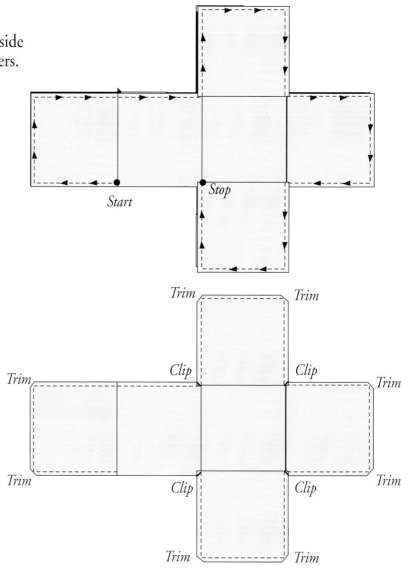

Completing the Box

1. Through the opening, slide the padded cardboard into the top of the box. Next insert cardboard into three of the sides and the bottom.

2. Last, place the remaining cardboard into the final side, adjacent to the opening.

3. With matching thread, hand sew the opening closed.

4. Thread large-eyed needle with ribbon. Pull a piece of ribbon through the corners of the box so the box will keep it's shape. Repeat process for all four corners.

5. Tie corners together.

6. Add loop and button for a closure to the top of the box.

Finishing the Quilt

Sewing the Quilt Top Together

1. Lay out all of the quilt blocks in the correct order.

2. Flip the second vertical row right sides together over the first row. Stack and sew.

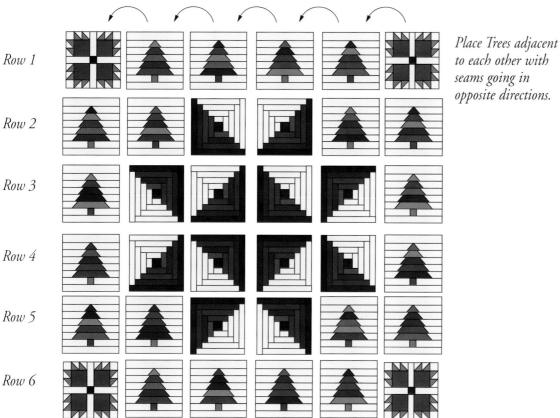

Row 1

Row 2

Row 3

Row 4

Row 5

Row 6

Place Trees adjacent to each other with seams going in opposite directions.

3. Continue sewing all blocks together in vertical rows. Press seam allowances in opposite directions.

4. Flip Row 1 over Row 2 with right sides together.
   Lock the pressed seams together.

5. Sew rows together, and press seams allowances towards even numbered rows.

Adding the Flying Geese Border

You need 104 Geese.

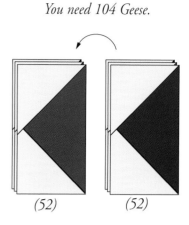

1. Separate Geese Patches into two stacks of 52 patches. All Geese should point toward the left.

(52) (52)

2. Assembly-line sew the two stacks right sides together to make 52 pairs of Geese Patches.

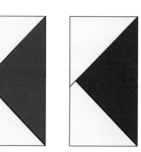

3. Set seams and press seam allowances towards the base of the sewn Geese Patch.

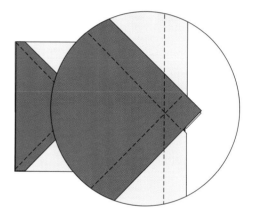

4. Set four pairs aside for the corners. Stack remaining 48 pairs into four stacks of 12. Assembly-line sew and press seam allowances toward the left.

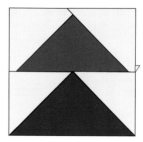

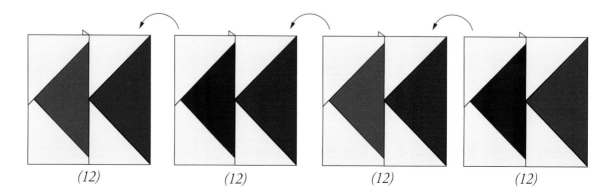

(12) (12) (12) (12)

5. Make three stacks of four Geese units. Assembly-line sew and press seam allowances toward the left. There are 24 Geese in each strip.

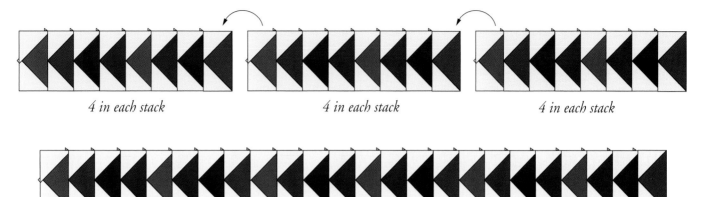

4 in each stack   *4 in each stack*   *4 in each stack*

6. Position Geese strips and 2-patch corners around pieced center. Match and pin sides Geese to the quilt. Four Geese equal one block. Sew.

Adding the Borders

Creativity in Border Sizes

Suggested border yardage and border examples are given for each quilt. However, you may wish to custom design the borders by changing the widths of the strips. This might change yardage for backing, binding, and batting.

When custom fitting the quilt, lay the top on your bed before adding the borders and backing. Measure to find how much border is needed to get the fit you want. Keep in mind that a large quilt will shrink approximately 3" in the length and width after machine quilting.

Piecing the Strips for Border and Binding

1. Stack and square off the ends of each strip, trimming away the selvage edges.

2. Seam the strips of each fabric into one long piece by assembly-line sewing.

   Lay the first strip right side up. Lay the second strip right sides to it. Backstitch, stitch the short ends together, and backstitch again.

   Take the strip on the top and fold it so the right side is up. Place the third strip right sides to it, backstitch and stitch, and backstitch again.

3. Clip the threads holding the strips together.

4. Press seams to one side.

Sewing the Borders to the Quilt Top

1. Measure down the center to find the length. Cut two side strips that measurement plus two inches.

2. Right sides together, match and pin the center of the strips to the center of the sides. Pin at ends, allowing an extra inch of border at each end. Pin intermittently. Sew with the quilt on top. Set and direct the seams, pressing toward the borders.

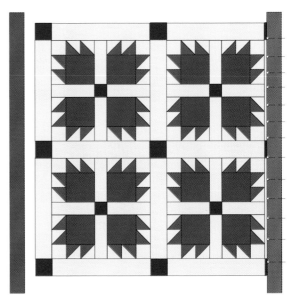

3. Square the ends even with the top and bottom of the quilt.

4. Measure the width across the center including newly added borders. Cut two strips that measurement plus two inches.

5. Right sides together, match and pin the center of the strips to the center of the top and bottom edges of the quilt. Pin at the ends, allowing an extra inch of border at both ends. Pin intermittently. Sew with the quilt on top.

6. Set and direct the seams, pressing toward the borders. Square the ends even with the side borders. Repeat these steps for additional borders.

Layering Quilt Top

1. Piece the backing yardage together for larger size quilts.

2. Stretch out the backing right side down on a table or floor. Tape down on a floor area or clamp onto a table with large binder clips.

3. Place and smooth out thin batting on top. Lay the quilt top right side up and centered on top of the batting. Completely smooth and stretch all layers until they are flat. Tape or clip securely.

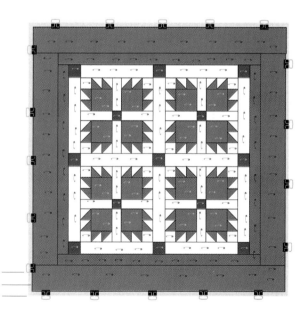

Clamps ———
Batting ———
Backing ———

Quick and Easy Safety Pinning

1. Place safety pins throughout the quilt away from the planned quilting lines. Begin pinning in the center and work to the outside, spacing them every 5".

2. Trim backing and batting to 2" on all sides.

Grasp the opened pin in your right hand and the pinning tool in your left hand. Push the pin through the three layers, and bring the tip of the pin back out. Catch the tip in the groove of the tool and allow point to extend far enough to push pin closed.

Straight Line Quilting

Use this technique for cross-hatch quilting or "stitching in the ditch" around the patchwork or through the borders.

Straight line quilting detail of Timberline

Machine Set Up

Place a walking foot attachment on your machine. Use invisible thread in the top of your machine and regular thread in the bobbin to match the backing. Loosen the top tension, and lengthen your stitch to 8 - 10 stitches per inch, or a #3 or #4 setting. Free arm machines need the "bed" placed for more surface area.

1. For cross-hatch quilting on background fabric, draw one straight line through the center with a silver or soapstone pencil, or piece of chalk.

2. Draw lines evenly spaced 2" apart from the center line in both directions.

3. Use the seam lines as a guide for "stitching in the ditch" around the patchwork and border.

Quilting with a Walking Foot

1. Roll the quilt tightly from the outside edge in toward middle. Hold this roll with clips or pins.

2. Slide this roll into the keyhole of the sewing machine.

3. Place the needle in the depth of the seam and pull up the bobbin thread. Stitch forward following the design. Pivot with the needle in the fabric. Lock the beginning and ending of each quilting line by backstitching.

4. Place your hands flat on both sides of the needle to form a hoop. Keep the quilt area flat and tight. If you need to ease in the top fabric, feed the quilt through the machine by pushing the layers of fabric and batting forward underneath the walking foot.

5. Unroll, roll, and machine quilt on all lines, sewing the length or width or diagonal of the quilt.

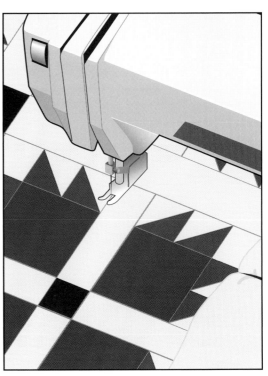

"stitching in the ditch" around the patchwork or through the borders

Free Motion Quilting

Use this technique to outline a stencil design in a background area, fill in background with stippling, or "stitch in the ditch" in the seams of the patchwork blocks. Feed dogs are disengaged, so large, bulky quilts can easily be stitched side to side as well as forward and backward with little manipulation.

Machine Set Up

Use a darning foot or spring needle, and drop the feed dogs or cover with a plate. No stitch length is required as you control the length. Use a fine needle and a little hole throat plate with a center needle position. Use invisible or regular thread in the top and regular thread to match the backing in the bobbin. Loosen the top tension if using invisible thread.

Stippling Your Quilt

Fill in background area with stippling or a meandering stitch.

1. Stitch into the center of the area with a worm-like stitch.

2. Do a curved turn and stitch back in the same direction loosely paralleling the worm-like stitch.

3. Continue to fill in the area with the stippling, being careful not to sew across a line of stitching.

Stippling detail of the Caribou Crossing

Adding the Binding

Use a walking foot attachment and regular thread on top and in the bobbin to match the binding. Use 10 stitches per inch, or #3 setting.

See page 122 to make one long binding strip.

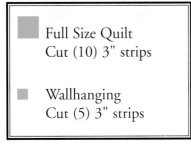

■ Full Size Quilt
Cut (10) 3" strips

■ Wallhanging
Cut (5) 3" strips

1. Press the binding strip in half lengthwise with right sides out.

2. Line up the raw edges of the folded binding with the raw edge of the quilt top at the middle of one side.

3. Begin sewing 4" from the end of the binding.

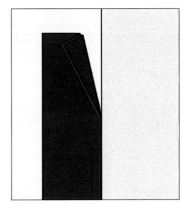

4. At the corner, stop the stitching ¼" from the edge with the needle in the fabric. Raise the presser foot and turn the quilt to the next side. Put the foot back down.

5. Sew backwards ¼" to the edge of the binding, raise the foot, and pull the quilt forward slightly.

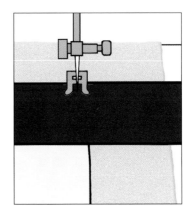

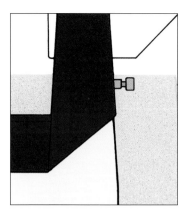

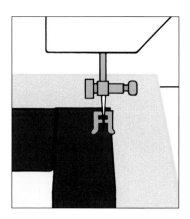

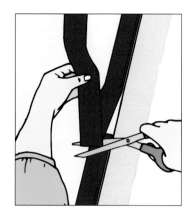

6. Fold the binding strip straight up on the diagonal. Fingerpress in the diagonal fold.

7. Fold the binding strip straight down with the diagonal fold underneath. Line up the top of the fold with the raw edge of the binding underneath.

8. Begin sewing from the corner.

9. Continue sewing and mitering the corners around the outside of the quilt.

10. Stop sewing 4" from where the ends will overlap.

11. Line up the two ends of binding. Trim the excess with a ½" overlap.

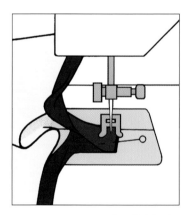

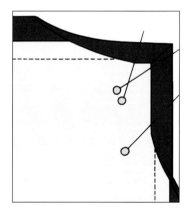

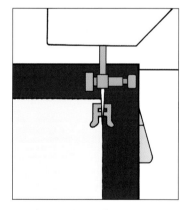

12. Open out the folded ends and pin right sides together. Sew a ¼" seam.

13. Continue to sew the binding in place.

14. Trim the batting and backing up to the raw edges of the binding.

15. Fold the binding to the backside of the quilt. Pin in place so that the folded edge on the binding covers the stitching line. Tuck in the excess fabric at each miter on the diagonal.

16. From the right side, "stitch in the ditch" using invisible thread on the right side, and a bobbin thread to match the binding on the back side.

    Optional: Slipstitch the binding in place by hand.

17. Sew an identification label on the backing.

Order Information

Quilt in a Day books offer a wide range of techniques and are directed toward a variety of skill levels. If you do not have a quilt shop in your area, you may write or call for a complete catalog and current price list of all books and patterns published by Quilt in a Day®, Inc.

Easy

Quilt in a Day Log Cabin
Irish Chain in a Day
Bits & Pieces Quilt
Trip Around the World Quilt
Heart's Delight Wallhanging
Scrap Quilt, Strips and Spider Webs
Rail Fence Quilt
Dresden Placemats
Flying Geese Quilt
Star for all Seasons Placemats
Winning Hand Quilt
Courthouse Steps Quilt
From Blocks to Quilt
Nana's Garden Quilt

Applique

Applique in a Day
Dresden Plate Quilt
Sunbonnet Sue Visits Quilt in a Day
Recycled Treasures
Country Cottages and More
Creating with Color
Spools & Tools Wallhanging
Dutch Windmills Quilt

Intermediate to Advanced

Trio of Treasured Quilts
Lover's Knot Quilt
Amish Quilt
May Basket Quilt
Morning Star Quilt
Friendship Quilt
Kaleidoscope Quilt
Machine Quilting Primer
Tulip Quilt
Star Log Cabin Quilt
Burgoyne Surrounded Quilt

Bird's Eye Quilt
Snowball Quilt
Tulip Table Runner
Jewel Box Quilt
Triple Irish Chain Quilts
Bears in the Woods

Holiday

Country Christmas
Bunnies & Blossoms
Patchwork Santa
Last Minute Gifts
Angel of Antiquity
Log Cabin Wreath Wallhanging
Log Cabin Christmas Tree Wallhanging
Country Flag
Lover's Knot Placemats

Sampler

The Sampler
Block Party Series 1, Quilter's Year
Block Party Series 2, Baskets & Flowers
Block Party Series 3, Quilters Almanac
Block Party Series 4, Christmas Traditions
Block Party Series 5, Pioneer Sampler

Angle Piecing

Diamond Log Cabin Tablecloth or Treeskirt
Pineapple Quilt
Blazing Star Tablecloth
Schoolhouse Quilt
Radiant Star Quilt

Quilt in a Day®, Inc. • 1955 Diamond Street, • San Marcos, CA 92069
Toll Free: 1 800 777-4852 • Fax: (760) 591-4424
Internet: www.quilt-in-a-day.com • 8 am to 5 pm Pacific Time